LIFTING THE VEIL
Esoteric Masonic Thought

Francesco Queirolo, *Il Disinganno*, Cappella Sansevero, Napoli

LIFTING THE VEIL
Esoteric Masonic Thought

Copyright © 2009 Lodgeroom International

Publisher: Promethean Genesis Publishing
PO Box 636
Lutz FL 33548-0636

All rights reserved under International and Pan-American Copy Right Conventions. No part of this publication may be reproduced, stored in retrieval system, transmitted or retransmitted in any form or by any means – electronic, mechanical, scanning, photographic, photocopying, recording, or otherwise – without the prior permission of the copyright owner.

ISBN-10: **0-9793070-4-X**
ISBN-13: **978-0-9793070-4-1**

First Printing, March 2009

Published in the United States of America
Book formatting by: Dr. John S. Nagy

Book available at: the Publisher's, or
http://www.lodgeroomuk.com/

The authors are available for speaking engagements. Please contact them through Lodgeroom International at:
http://www.lodgeroomuk.com/

FOREWORD

Two years ago, Robert Theron Dunn ("Theron"), Bill McElligott and I discussed how to help the American Brethren who set up "Traditional Obedience" lodges, and others who merely desired to improve their esoteric knowledge.

Myself, I am an Italian Freemason, and my lodge runs its business with the AASR ritual. Therefore, there are some differences as far as the ritual is concerned. I add that Italy is, at an esoteric level, the heir of the mysteries practiced in the Mediterranean area years ago, especially in Greece. There is a different mentality involved and different practices. To Masons who don't practice within Italy, some of our rituals can appear quite weird, if they are unexplained and not understood.

Our lodge involves our new members in an educational process from the start. We provide new members with a booklet containing various informative articles. These articles cover both the general aspects of Freemasonry and the most common symbols which man finds in our Temple.

Based on what I shared about our provided materials, Theron proposed we should to do the same for the benefit of the English speaking Masonic world. We all agreed and I rolled up my sleeves and began writing from the Italian Masonic viewpoint. At the same time, I asked some American and Australian Brethren to deliver their articles on the specific aspects of their ritual. Let me underline that they all complied with my request with much enthusiasm, competence and Brotherly love.

This booklet before you is an attempt to explain various Masonic symbols in esoteric terms. As far as it is possible, the authors have avoided any "moral" interpretation. Esotericism is not a doctrine; it is a method, which leads men to look deeper into themselves, firstly, then after to the surrounding environment and eventually to the divine. By so doing, they come to realize that they are part of the whole. In addition, they also come to understand the reason for which ancient alchemists used to say "As above, so below."

Initiates deepen their esoteric knowledge by rites and symbols: when man deals with the Transcendent, words are never adequate. On this purpose, Dante perspicuously wrote, "Passing beyond the human cannot be worded".[1]

Unexpectedly, Theron passed away on the 13th of May in 2008. My friend and Brother who urged me to fulfill this task and encouraging me to go beyond any difficulties, is no more with us in person. He is still part of our "chain" in another form, though.

Theron, my Brother, go on helping us through your spiritual assistance; I dedicate this work to your beloved memory, which time will never erase. *Vivat!*

Milano, *Vernal Solstice* 2008

Giovanni Lombardo

---

[1] *Comedy*, Paradiso, I, 70

Esoteric Masonic Thought

DEDICATION

In Loving Memory

ROBERT THERON DUNN
(February 1, 1957 - May 13, 2008)

*It's not about me changing them,
it's about me changing me!*

Bro. Theron Dunn

TABLE OF CONTENTS

FOREWORD II
DEDICATION IV
ON TOLERANCE AND INTOLERANCE: ONE MASON'S PERSPECTIVE 1
SIMPLY, WHAT IS ESOTERICISM 7
INITIATION 13
WHY IS RITUAL IMPORTANT TO FREEMASONRY? 19
JUST A FEW WORDS ON RITUAL 23
ON THE ORIGINS OF FREEMASONIC RITUAL 26
THE INITIATE'S WORK 35
THE INITIATIC SECRET 39
THE SYMBOL 43
THE SYMBOL AND ITS FUNCTION 46
THE ASHLAR UNFOLDED 48
THE SILENCE OF THE INITIATE 53
THE CHAMBER OF REFLECTION 61
ORIENTATIONS AND PERAMBULATIONS 73
SQUARE AND COMPASSES 79
THE TESSELLATED PAVEMENT 83
THE THREE PILLARS 88
THE TRACING BOARD 101
GODS IN LODGE 104
THE BLAZING STAR 113
THE POINT WITHIN THE CIRCLE 115
WHAT IS AN EGREGORE? 127
THE CHAIN OF UNION 133
THE MASONIC DRESS 138

ON TOLERANCE AND INTOLERANCE: ONE MASON'S PERSPECTIVE

By: R. Theron Dunn

One of the principle teachings of Freemasonry is tolerance. We don't speak of it in lodge much, but it is inherent in the way a lodge operates, it is custom. The most "visible" evidence of tolerance in lodge is the unwritten custom of not allowing proselytizing or the discussion of politics.

The teachings on prudence, justice and temperance, though, it could be argued, are directly related to tolerance, as is brotherly love. But the most definitive discussion on tolerance can be found in Morals and Dogma by Wr. Br. Albert Pike, Sovereign Grand Commander of the Ancient and Accepted Scottish Rite, Southern Jurisdiction.

> ...it (toleration) inculcates in the strongest manner that great leading idea of the Ancient Art, that a belief in the one True God, and a moral and virtuous life, constitute the only religious requisites needed to enable a man to be a Mason.
>
> Masonry has ever the most vivid remembrance of the terrible and artificial torments that were used to put down new forms of religion or extinguish the old. It sees with the eye of memory the ruthless extermination of all the people of all sexes and ages, because it was their misfortune not to know the God of the Hebrews, or to worship Him under the wrong name, by the savage troops of Moses and Joshua. It sees the thumb-screws and the racks, the whip, the gallows, and the stake, the victims of Diocletian and Alva, the miserable Covenanters, the Non-Conformists, Servetus burned, and the unoffending Quaker hung. It sees Cranmer hold his arm, now no longer erring, in the flame until the hand drops off in the consuming heat. It sees the persecutions of Peter and

Paul, the martyrdom of Stephen, the trials of Ignatius, Polycarp, Justin, and Irenæus; and then in turn the sufferings of the wretched Pagans under the Christian Emperors, as of the Papists in Ireland and under Elizabeth and the bloated Henry. The Roman Virgin naked before the hungry lions; young Margaret Graham tied to a stake at low-water mark, and there left to drown, singing hymns to God until the savage waters broke over her head; and all that in all ages have suffered by hunger and nakedness, peril and prison, the rack, the stake, and the sword, - it sees them all, and shudders at the long roll of human atrocities. And it sees also the oppression still practiced in the name of religion - men shot in a Christian jail in Christian Italy for reading the Christian Bible; in almost every Christian State, laws forbidding freedom of speech on matters relating to Christianity; and the gallows reaching its arm over the pulpit.

No man truly obeys the Masonic law who merely tolerates those whose religious opinions are opposed to his own. Every man's opinions are his own private property, and the rights of all men to maintain each his own are perfectly equal. Merely to tolerate, to bear with an opposing opinion, is to assume it to be heretical; and assert the right to persecute, if we would; and claim our toleration of it as a merit. The Mason's creed goes further than that. No man, it holds, has any right in any way to interfere with the religious belief of another.

It appears that, in Wr. Pike's opinion, we are called upon as Masons to demonstrate more than simple toleration. But, what does that mean?

Merriam-Webster defines To Tolerate as:
... to endure, o put up with; akin to Old English tholian to bear, Latin tollere to lift up, la-

tus carried (suppletive past participle of ferre), Greek tlenai to bear
1 : to exhibit physiological tolerance for (as a drug)
2 a : to suffer to be or to be done without prohibition, hindrance, or contradiction b : to put up with

To endure... to put up with... to suffer it to be done without prohibition... so, in essence, to simply tolerate something is to endure it in silence. That is brotherly?

But what is the next level? If we go beyond simple toleration, where are we? Acceptance? Well, that certainly seems correct, so let's examine acceptance for a moment.

Merriam-Webster defines to Accept as:

1 a : to receive willingly <accept a gift> b : to be able or designed to take or hold (something applied or added) <a surface that will not accept ink>

2 : to give admittance or approval to <accept her as one of the grup>

3 a : to endure without protest or reaction <accept poor living conditions> b : to regard as proper, normal, or inevitable <the idea is widely accepted> c : to recognize as true : BELIEVE <refused to accept the explanation>

4 a : to make a favorable response to <accept an offer> b : to agree to undertake (a responsibility) <accept a job>

5 : to assume an obligation to pay; also : to take in payment <we don't accept personal checks>

6 : to receive (a legislative report) officially intransitive senses : to receive favorably something offered

To give admittance or approval to... to endure without protest or reaction... neither separately is the correct Masonic position, but together, these two might suffice. Two brothers may vehemently disagree on a subject, but if each brother accepts the other's **right** to that opinion and the brother's **right** to believe differently, then we are closer to the Masonic ideal.

This is not to say that we must each accept the others POSITION, for we do have right to our own thoughts, and it could be argued that it is quintessentially Masonic for brothers to work out for themselves that which is right, fit, mete and proper. It is, however, entirely unmasonic to try to suppress a brother for having a differing opinion. It is wrong to go out and try to change a brother's opinion, or to convert him.

Discussion of issues and the exchange of positions, while it may seem contradictory, is not intolerant of non accepting, for it is by the exchange of ideas and thoughts that we all grow. However, pushing your onto a brother is intolerant… for instance, the prohibition against proselytizing in lodge is quintessentially a Masonic virtue, for if a brother is interested in your position on religion, he will ask… outside of lodge.

But the whole issue of religion and tolerance is a thorny one. I recently made the point to a brother that preaching to someone, going door to door, bracing them in the workplace or in the street, or sending "missionaries" to another country is, on its face, intolerant. Masonically, it is intolerant, for it is a failure to accept the other person's beliefs (or lack thereof), and a pushing of one person's opinion onto another.

If group A sends people door to door to "share" their version of faith, those folks going door to door are intruding (literally trespassing) to push their views, and are, by definition, being intolerant of the views held by the people they are intruding upon. If a group sends people to another country to "feed and clothe the poor", and of course, share their faith with them, those people are being intolerant of the beliefs and customs of the people they are feeding and clothing.

If they were truly interested in just feeding and clothing, they wouldn't take as many holy books with them as potatoes...

The difference between *mere toleration* and acceptance of another's right to his views is a simple matter of intent. If you go to a man and ask him his opinion on a subject, be it religion or politics or the shape of the clouds in the sky *with the intent of sharing with him your own view* then you are not being tolerant of his views.

This is an extreme interpretation to make a point, but it is no less true for that. Some feel it is the nature of their religion, the call of their faith, to share with everyone the nature of that faith. Wonderful, however, doing that is a manifest demonstration of intolerance... done with the best of intentions.

Another example of this is the War Between the North and the South here in the United States in the 1860's. Examples abound of Masons on each side of the war, stopping to hold joint funeral services for fallen brothers, to hold out a Masonic lodge from being burned or looted, to give shelter or forbearance to a brother... **during a shooting war**. THAT was true Masonry.

Today, we see a definite lack of tolerance in the lodge. There are issues that have come up, changes in process and procedures of varying natures. As usual, there is one group championing the change, and as usual, there is a group the opposes the change, and there is always they third group that really don't care and just want to get to the coffee and donuts.

Under true Masonic tolerance, we would accept each other's right to have the opinion(s) and move on. Unfortunately, we see one side or the other trying to shut up the dissenters. There are claims of divisiveness, "Masonic Civil War", splitting the craft etc etc as rhetoric to stop one side from holding their own opinions.

Masonic teaching would have us accept the other opinion, and the each other's right to have those opinions, and seek common ground, but that is not happening. Instead, we see retrenchment, and, frankly, resentment. The issue doesn't matter, there are several of them facing us today. The Masonic way would be to work together instead of trying to win at all costs. As one man wrote, it is better to have half a pie than no pie at all... that is acceptance.

Masonically, it is not about winning, or shouldn't be... oh, we have elections, and we have moderated debate in lodge over issues, decorous and brotherly... mostly. Then we vote, and the vote should end the discussion... but it often turns into more than that after the election is done.

So, what is Masonic tolerance? In reality, it *should* be, in this mason's opinion about brothers seeking how best to work and *best agree*. It should be about accepting our brothers for who they are and what their faith is, and how we can best learn to be better men before g-d and our fellow men.

No man truly obeys the Masonic law who merely tolerates those whose opinions are opposed to his own.

SIMPLY, WHAT IS ESOTERICISM

By: Athos A. Altomonte

Q: *«I hope you won't laugh at my question: what exactly is esotericism? If you can answer please do it in a way a sixteen year old boy can understand it.*

P.S. if you think I'm a burden for the list because of my ignorance you can cancel me, although I would be disappointed. Thank you very much, V. G.»

A: I have always stuck to the scale of values that I have been taught which, in the respect of economic laws, lavishes the maximum in the minimum and the minimum in the maximum. I'll explain myself.

The time, the abilities and the energy that an instructor directs to his work are considered a fruitful investment. This work is mainly directed to the divulgence of initiatory principles meant for the education of the aspirants. The more fruitful is the work, the more profitable is the investment. The result, though, will depend on both the protagonists, that are the pupil and the instructor.

Initiatory education is not the only one to inspire more attention to the least expert rather than to the oldest, which are maybe standing still at the post of mundane habits. It is difficult for the latter to accept willingly to correct the preconceived ideas they have been "feeding on", originated by a derivate culture lacking in personal experience. Furthermore, every situation of prejudice is created by choice and not by chance.

Certainly to explain what esotericism is to a sixteen year old boy is a stimulating trial; but sixteen year olds must grow as well, therefore I'd start saying to this sixteen year old that **esotericism is a method of enquiry and not a philosophy.**

It is a precious method if it is used by able researchers to "strip" the object of study from exterior covers (formal or literal meanings) up to reach its deep meaning.

I am talking about **the soul of the meaning and not the apparent meaning** of the word, the idea, the symbol or any identity we are supposed to discover.

The esoterical enquiry starts from the exterior "covers" and penetrates up to reaching the central nucleus of the idea, which is its soul. The method of research is similar to peel an onion that, skin after skin, is "stripped" of its external covers and makes visible the essential part of the inner nucleus and by analogy, the **center of the system.**

On Esonet there are plenty of works dealing with esotericism, from the most classic one to the scientific one.

An example of how to "strip" a symbol down to "touch" its soul, that is the radical meaning that is its cause and fundament, is the work: *"The Mysteries of the Builders"* where chapter after chapter, are taken back to life the invisible meanings of the Cathedral (the Sephirotic Tree and the cosmic Man crucified in the four elements of the matter). It is also discovered that the "signs" marked on the Cathedrals are the same that give form to the internal spaces of the Masonic Temples.

Before talking about esotericism, though, we must understand how the esoterical research occurs; how we can remove skin after skin and "reveal" the hidden meaning of what we want to know.

The core of the matter is in the words **to analyze and to link**, which are the pillars of esotericism and explain a method that **analyzes facts and circumstances through analogy and correspondences.**

The word esotericism derives from the Greek word *esoterikós* that means inner and therefore looking inside. There is a similar word in Latin: *intelligere* (to know the principle of things – op. cit. C. Vallaturi, C. Durando) from which derives *intelligentia* (the noblest faculty of the soul – op. cit. C. Vallaturi, C. Durando) which is not *learning by heart* (**sciolism**) but the ability to understand the inner (occult) sense of what is perceived, seen, touched and heard.

The esoterical enquiry doesn't involve only abstract concepts or symbols, but it applies to the most refined subject for research as well: the extraordinary **living symbol** that is a human being.

To start a deep research on a living symbol (**archetypical Man**) means to find an answer that will have to be correct under the scientific profile as well, at least until we cross the metaphysical boundary.

The reason for this is that **esotericism is not a result of old tales neither of obscure medieval eccentricities**, but an instrument for enquiry rooted into the initiatory science.

V.I.T.R.I.O.L. – *Visita Interiora Terrae Rectificando Invenies Occultum Lapidem.* Visit the Inside of (your) Earth and Rectifying (correcting yourself) you will Find the Occult Stone (the soul).

Knowing the most secret (deep) part of a person means to reach the aura (Light) of his soul.

The esoterical representation of this inner journey is a Labyrinth.

The Labyrinth with its many aspects represents the destiny and the paths that are the lives of individual's commitment or journey.

All the paths or roads converge to the center but, like in life, many paths (decided experiences) are dead end roads and don't lead anywhere. Others, on the other hand, intersect with other paths or roads and allow the "traveler" to advance.

The paths or roads represent the possibility of choice. In the choice (see the Art to decide) everyone will be able to throw his experiences, his common sense or, on the contrary, all his foolishness; he is free to try, to advance, to stop or to fail.

Looking at the East, I'd say that the Labyrinth is a wonderful representation of the principle of the Karma. The symbol that better shows the difference between **"free choice"**, empirical and casual, and **Free Will.**

Free Will, in simple words, is the result of inner illumination (**Initiation**) that is produced thanks to the contact between soul and personality.

Therefore on the flat part of the floor (**physical life**) there isn't a chance for Free Will, which is generated by a status of conscience (**consciousness**) of a superior order, reached (**expansion of conscience**) after we are elevated on the vertical path, which represents the ascent to the plane of spiritual **conscience**, seat of the soul.

The principle of light-shadow (black and white) *divides but at the same time joins* the material and the spiritual planes; it is given by the "comparison" (allow me this daring word) between the spiritual nucleus (the soul) that is visible as Light in the most external and dense planes, and the physical personality, the concrete mind that is its shadow.

Here originates the saying that advices the physical mind, the shadow, to help intellectual modesty, because every thought it has is still lacking of the light of the soul (illumination).

This as well, like any other symbology, veils the approach to a method for inner growth that I can certainly define rational and scientific.

There are many horizontal entrances to the Labyrinth, but there is only one exit and it is a vertical one. Therefore we can only get out by "flying"; that is by rising from the floor of material life. This can happen only by subliming oneself, the thoughts of the personal self and personality.

The metaphor of hovering, the ascent to the sky, the wings and the flight, mentioned in the Caduceus of Hermes as well, hides the diagram to complete the initiatory journey, reach the "liberation" from earthly bonds (such as passion) and accomplish the real initiation.

Resuming: the Labyrinth symbolizes the flat part of the initiatory dilemma (the concrete conscience) that under the form of a spiral evolves towards the top (the inner sky).

The ascent (the spiral) as well is represented by the symbol of an inner Mountain (See Plato and Dante) that must be climbed. We can decide to do it in several ways.

One way is the large path, more comfortable, sure but slow. The other way is the narrow path, arduous and risky, but quick.

This metaphor refers to the inner journey that every postulant carries out in the search for initiation.

We still have to establish what initiation is and what its goal is. It is not to inflate with pride the personal self (concrete mind) as it happens in exoterical structures that represent initiation in a symbolical, and therefore only apparent shape.

It is necessary to make a distinction here. Real Initiation is not a simple recognition amongst peers but the result of the transmutation (*metamòrphosis*) in the physical conscience of the concrete mind of the initiate, in communion or re-joining with its subtle counterpart.

Modern science calls this part super-conscious.

The journey through the Labyrinth (physical existence) and the re-ascent towards the high (inner and subtle) planes of the inner Mountain (the destiny) is the metaphor of the journey that the physical conscience (personal self) does in order to reach the counterpart of itself to a superior spiral (superior Ego).

The perception of oneself "enters" the physical body through senses and must be able to coherently dominate the impulsive, physical and emotional part.

Its journey continues through the development of the several planes of the physical mind and builds the conscience bridge that joins it to that part of superior (subtle) conscience called soul.

We can now remind you of the 12 eastern Yogas, which Esonet presented an article about; they represent as many paths or means, to lead the several parts of the physical conscience (personal self) towards the last synthesis (Buddhi), that is the Chakra of the head in which the soul appears (Atmá).

Once again, if we are able to read them, the aspects of the East and the West match.

It is taught that the inner journey is guided by a higher Brother. An expert Brother that knows the path *because he has covered it successfully many times.*

The guide is the instructor that leads the pupil in his initiatory journey. He "holds his hand" on the threshold of the physical plane and takes him backwards in himself. Going up by planes (impulses, emotions, feelings, up to the formulation of abstract ideas) at the presence of the Ego to which he entrusts him because his task ends there.

At that point, though, the journey can continue; not as instructor and pupil, though, but as Fellow Travelers because the goal to be reached is the same.

INITIATION

By: Bruce Nevin

An initiation is a beginning.

Every initiation has an outward aspect carried out by particular people, with you, at a certain time and place. At the same time, there is always an interior aspect taking place within you. The inner initiation is the true significance of the outer events, and is their purpose or aim.

The outward ritual is almost always imperfect. One person may fumble some words or even omit whole paragraphs. Floor work may stumble, ritual actions may be malformed, jogged out of place, or forgotten. And even if the officers perform flawlessly, your perception of the ritual as the initiate is incomplete. The very meanings of the words are not immediately available to you, much less the symbolism.

Later, as you witness from the sidelines the ritual being performed with new initiates, the significance of different aspects opens to you more and more. Each such witnessing furthers your inward initiation.

The more you involve yourself as a participant, the more light is opened to you; or, more truly, the more you open to the light.

The purpose of initiation is to change people—to make good men better, as we say. Ritual works within you because your subconscious mind is always amenable to suggestion. Since it is your subconscious mind that builds and daily reconstitutes what you are as a person, that little word "always" is worthy of your careful consideration. Your subconscious mind may take absolutely anything that you experience or do or say or think as a suggestion, on the basis of which she changes the way you are constituted as a person. Feelings make thoughts, thoughts form words, words lead to actions, actions form into habits, habits congeal as character. And there you are.

The philosopher Søren Kierkegaard wrote a small book titled *Purity of Heart is to Will One Thing*. What is it to purify the heart, and so to will one thing? Surely, it is to know what you want. What is your heart's desire? But that simple question "what do you want?" is much easier to ask than to answer.

We all have so many desires for and against this and that, jostling and competing with one another. We are like young Al Addin, who found an old lamp from which, when he rubbed to clean it, emerged a powerful Jinn. Only when we make a wish, a suggestion to our subconscious, and the spirit turns to do our bidding, another voice within cries "No, wait!" and substitutes a different wish. No sooner does the Jinn turned to the task than there is another wish, and then another, and so that mighty servant can only spin around like a whirlwind, doing nothing productive and maybe even knocking things over by accident.

All these competing voices, where do they come from? All our lives we have collected shoulds and shouldn'ts, musts and cannots, like barnacles. Advertising and media suggest that we will feel happy and fulfilled if we have this or that possession to represent ourselves to others with the trappings of style and success. That smiling man, that smooth-skinned, poised woman, they cannot possibly suffer the frustrations and petty conflicts that I have to deal with, and if I were successful like them it would all be smooth sailing for me too!

We know all about these tricks of the PR game consciously, intellectually, but our subconscious mind is naïve, like a child within us. We have to stop letting just every suggestion in willy-nilly. To do that requires a working relationship with your subconscious.

That's not quite like rubbing dirt off an old lamp. It's more like a courtship. It takes time, and persistence, and you have to care. This is how the fox put it to the little prince:

"Please—tame me!" he said.

"I want to, very much," the little prince replied. *"But I have not much time. I have friends to discover, and a great many things to understand."*

"One only understands the things that one tames," said the fox. *"Men have no time to understand anything. They buy things already made at the shops. But there is no shop anywhere where one can buy friendship, and so men have no friends any more. If you want a friend, tame me . . ."*

What does that mean—'tame'?"

"It is an act too often neglected," said the fox. *"It means to establish ties."*

. . .

"What must I do, to tame you?" asked the little prince.

"You must be very patient," replied the fox. *"First you will sit down at a little distance from me—like that—in the grass. I shall look at you out of the corner of my eye, and you will say nothing. Words are the source of misunderstandings. But you will sit a little closer to me, every day . . ."*

The next day the little prince came back.

"It would have been better to come back at the same hour," said the fox. *"If, for example, you come at four o'clock in the afternoon, then at three o'clock I shall begin to be happy. I shall feel happier and happier as the hour advances. At four o'clock, I shall already be worrying and jumping about. I shall show you how happy I am! But if you come at just any time, I shall never know at what hour my heart is to be ready to greet you . . . One must observe the proper rites . . ."*

"What is a rite?" asked the little prince.[1]

What is a rite? What is a ritual? Surely at the least it is something done at a regular time and place, in the same way each time. But that is not enough. Those words are enough to describe mere habit.

---

[1] *The Little Prince* by Antoine de Saint-Exupéry. This little book for children has more to say to us than appears on the surface. See for example *L'ésotérisme du Petit Prince de Saint-Exupéry*, by Emmanuel-Yves Monin

Masonry communicates by symbol and allegory. What does this mean? Even though words are spoken in the ritual, they refer to symbols which communicate nonverbally. We must read them the way illiterate people read stained glass and statuary in the middle ages. Our rituals represent to us, duly assembled with our brethren, what it is to be a Mason. They display a pattern on the trestle board. These symbolic and allegorical representations are suggestive. As we pay attention to our Masonic rituals (repeatedly, consistently in certain places and at certain regular times), "workmen" of the subconscious reconstitute us according to that pattern, building the temple not made with hands.

Symbols and allegories provoke thought. Their interpretation is not always obvious at a conscious level. For example, the plumb teaches us to be upright, and the level teaches us to deal in all matters on the level with our fellows. But can't a stiff rectitude foster disharmony? Don't you have to go along to get along? Do you perhaps fear being thought a stiff-necked moralizing prig? Think about that felt conflict, for we shall return to it presently. And now consider the example before us of Hiram holding to moral principle even to death, and yet all the while acting entirely on the level with his attackers, not supercilious or aloof in his station. He simply restated the conditions for their advancement, which they well knew, and even gave positive assurance that they would receive what they wished when they met the requirement for "regular and upright conduct."

While we are in training, moral principles are stated prescriptively, as guidelines that prescribe what we should and should not do. As our inward initiation progresses, those same statements of moral principle become descriptive. Instead of being rules by which we should constrain our behavior, they flow naturally from our inner nature. And this is not by adding them to our inner nature. That true inner nature is within you all along, obscured only by a clutter of conflicting suggestions to your subconscious mind. The transition from rough ashlar to perfect ashlar is accomplished by removing what is unneeded.

The seeming conflict between rectitude and acting on the level, those moral principles that are represented emblematically by the plumb and the level, arises out of our fear of what others might think of us. With the progress of our inward initiation, our intuitions of the thoughts and feelings of our fellows ripen, by a winding way, from apprehension to empathy, from conformity to compassion, and rather than governing, they inform.

To an extent this will happen slowly over time if you merely persist in sitting through the ritual. You are well advised, however, to take matters in hand and participate more actively in your own advancement. Memorizing ritual is a first stage. Sub-consciousness in a fundamental aspect is a storehouse of memory. To memorize the words, you must open a conversation with your subconscious mind. Make her acquaintance. She works by association. Be alert, and she will offer you associative clues that will help you to remember. Move your body and enact the words in posture and gesture. The words and images of ritual provoke thought and raise questions in your mind. Write these down, and when you retire at night spend a few moments pondering them. Then when you awaken in the morning, look again and see if some new insights have been offered to you from within. As you learn, think about how to apply those meanings to situations in your daily life. At first you will recognize practical applications only retrospectively as you think back over the events of the day and week. With time and persistence, the principles that you imbibe from Masonic ritual begin to inform your responses. Pay attention. Listen to what comes from within. This is intuition: inner tuition, teaching from within you, from the same teachers who have guided Masons from time beyond memory.

As you watch and listen from the sidelines, as you attend Lodge of Instruction, as you go to rehearsals, even if only to observe and help when needed, as you move through the chairs enacting your part with the others, each part in turn— by virtue of such "homework," every time the outer initiation comes around the circle it is at a new level of a waxing spiral of growth. Each time, new disclosures open to you, new insight into the significance of the words, and beyond words the significance of the actions, the floor work, the lights, ornaments, jewels, furniture, implements, the officers and their roles—all aspects of the ritual progressively light up with meaning, and shed light each on the others. As that light brightens and spreads within you, all that is not of that light naturally falls away, as shadows, and the light spreads outwardly in all your relations with your fellows, easily, as water flows. This is the progress of your inner initiation, and the true meaning and purpose of the outer.

WHY IS RITUAL IMPORTANT TO FREEMASONRY?

By: R. Theron Dunn

First, this is not going to be an article about Masonic ritual, I do have an obligation to maintain. However, this this will examine ritual as it pertains to Freemasonry. Please, read on and let me know what you think about ritual. The next blog entry will discuss the probably source(s) of Masonic ritual.

As always when discussing a subject of import, let's start off with a definition and progress in the examination. So, what IS a ritual:

A ritual is a set of actions, often thought to have symbolic value, the performance of which is usually prescribed by a religion or by the traditions of a community by religious or political laws because of the perceived efficacy of those actions.

A ritual may be performed at regular intervals, or on specific occasions, or at the discretion of individuals or communities. It may be performed by a single individual, by a group, or by the entire community; in arbitrary places, or in places especially reserved for it; either in public, in private, or before specific people. A ritual may be restricted to a certain subset of the community, and may enable or underscore the passage between religious or social states.

The purposes of rituals are varied; they include compliance with religious obligations or ideals, satisfaction of spiritual or emotional needs of the practitioners, strengthening of social bonds, demonstration of respect or submission, stating one's affiliation, obtaining social acceptance or approval for some event — or, sometimes, just for the pleasure of the ritual itself.

Rituals of various kinds are a feature of almost all known human societies, past or present. They include not only the various worship rites and sacraments of organized religions and cults, but also the rites of passage of certain societies, oaths of allegiance, coronations, and presidential inaugurations, marriages and funerals, school "rush" traditions and graduations, club meetings, sports events, Halloween parties and veteran parades, Christmas shopping, and more. Many activities that are ostensibly performed for concrete purposes, such as jury trials, execution of criminals, and scientific symposia, are loaded with purely symbolic actions prescribed by regulations or tradition, and thus partly ritualistic in nature. Even common actions like handshaking and saying hello are rituals.

In any case, an essential feature of a ritual is that the actions and their symbolism are not arbitrarily chosen by the performers, nor dictated by logic or necessity, but either are prescribed and imposed upon the performers by some external source or are inherited unconsciously from social traditions.[1]

So, it's a set of actions though to have symbolic value that are traditional and are not arbitrarily chosen by the performers. Sounds a lot like Freemasonic ritual so far. Joseph Campbell said:

«A ritual is the enactment of a myth. And through the enactment it brings to mind the implications of the life act that you are engaged in ... But you don't know what you're doing unless you think about it. That's what a ritual does. It give you an occasion to realize what you're doing so that you're participating in the inevitable energy of life in its exchanges. That's what rituals are for; you do things with intention, and not just in the animal way, ravenously, without knowing what you're doing.»[2]

Enactment of a myth, symbolism, imposed on the performers. Now that we have defined what ritual is, now we should begin to look at the place ritual has in Freemasonry, and what it does for the craft.

---

[1] Wikipedia – English: http://en.wikipedia.org/wiki/Ritual 2/26/08
[2] *Mythic Reflections, Thoughts on myth, spirit, and our times an interview with Joseph Campbell, by Tom Collins*, One of the articles in The New Story (IC#12), Winter 1985/86, Page 52 Copyright (c)1986, 1997 by Context Institute.

One thing that should be noted is that while ritual is the foundational means by which we form Masons from the profanes of the world, it is not the *only* means of Masonic formation. Yet, in writing that, we must realize that it is the ritual that opens the door, and it is the ritual the effects the fundamental change in the psyche which makes a man a Mason. There are some men that have been made a Mason in a single day, and while they are good men, true brothers, it is the opinion of this author that such brothers have been robbed of a valuable and life changing experience.

Are these brothers any less Masons for not having personally experienced the ritual? No, of course not, most of them are active, wonderful brothers. None the less, the manner of their formation took away from them a fundamental awakening of the spirit which they may only achieve with difficult work and contemplation.

It is NOT the intent of this article to discuss the relative merits of one day conferrals, however, but no discussion of the importance of the ritual in the formation of a mason would be complete without at least a nod in the direction of this subject.

Ritual teaches fundamental lessons through symbols, on a subconscious level. This is a very powerful teaching tool! Masonry is something slightly different to every man, yet the fundamental truths are always there, and it is the ritual which speaks to the unconscious mind, which slips the fundamental truths of Freemasonry past the conscious defenses and makes fundamental and substantive changes.

So, why ritual? Again, quoting Joseph Campbell:

«It has always been the prime function of mythology and rite to supply the symbols that carry the human spirit forward, in counteraction to those other constant human fantasies that tend to tie it back.»[3]

---

[3] *The Hero With A Thousand Faces*, Joseph Campbell, Bollingen Series XVII, Princeton University Press, 1973, pp 11

Ritual then is the tool which speaks directly to the spirit, it is the three distinct knocks upon the portals of the spirit which cause the doors to open and spiritual eye to open and see more than the material world. By this awakening, we use the spiritual eye (reflected in our lodges as the "All Seeing Eye") to behold Jacob's Ladder, which rises from the material plane to the spiritual plane, and upon which we place our first foot, symbolically, in the Entered Apprentice Degree.

Without the Ritual, Freemasonry would just be another frat club, and would offer nothing more than the Moose or Elks or Eagles... material charity without a spiritual change.

JUST A FEW WORDS ON RITUAL

By: Giovanni Lombardo

> Ritual is an art, the art of religion. Art is the outward material expression of ideas intellectually held and emotionally felt. Ritual art is concerned with the expression of those ideas and feelings which are specifically called religious. It is a mode by which religious truth is presented, and made intelligible in material forms and symbols to the mind. It appeals to all natures passionately sensible of that Beauty in which, to some, God most manifests Himself. But it is more than this. For it is the means by which the mind is transformed and purified...
> (Arthur Avalon, *Shakti and Shâkta*)

* * *

In the early days of my Masonic life I remember an old, grumpy Brother in my lodge. He paid a lot of attention to the ritual, and if a Brother made a mistake, he waited till the closing and then jumped the poor brother, shouting «This is not the Rotary club!»

Setting aside any paranoid attitudes, rite and symbol are nevertheless an essential part of any initiatory context. Even more, the rite itself is a symbol, an "acted symbol", as Bro. Guénon defined it.

Unfortunately, because of either negligence or ignorance, it often happens that nobody explains the deep meaning of the ritual to the candidate (or the brethren for that matter), so it is neither understood nor lived. It remains in the corner, like a cumbersome trimming, that is taken out only on special occasions, and not being understood, provokes nothing but clumsiness and embarrassment.

It is not the purpose of this article to take a position about a particular ritual, be it Scottish, York, English or French. In a so widespread a communion as Freemasonry, being spread all over the world, it is unavoidable - and perhaps good, too - that the rituals show traces of the particular history attitudes of each country. We will, therefore focus more generally on rituality's meaning and purpose, which will be a greater service to the Craft.

The ritual can be examined from various perspectives. The first is that of purification. Through the ritual the brethren get rid of his "metals" by coming ritually in to the Temple. It is for this reason that it is important for the brethren to gather together fraternally for at least thirty minutes before starting the ritual work.

We should do this to remove ourselves from the profane world, so the brethren can join informally to wake the egregore of the lodge. This awakening, or quickening acts to shed the profane world and bring them gradually into the special atmosphere, full of a mix of rational and sacred, both united by the fraternal love.

The second perspective is that of consciousness-raising. By acting ritually, repeating words and gestures, being attentive so everything is "upright and perfect", each Brother becomes aware of his being, of his life which goes through in a way quite different from the profane one. With awareness comes knowledge. To study symbols with companions who strive to ignore their differences, to work together for a common goal, improves the whole humankind.

The third perspective is the creative one. To work ritually is tantamount to re-creating, by repeating a cosmogony in smaller terms. This entails the pass from *kaos* to *kosmos*, from chaos to order - the word "rite" stemming from Sanskrit *rta*, which means "complying with the order".

To create order, a scale of values needed, to differentiate the "wheat from chaff". In creating order out of the confusion which any novices feels, masons are forced to reassess their behaviour and old values which they have abandoned but not yet replaced. The inner path is long and gradual and there are no shortcuts. Patience and persistence in building the inner "edifice", which is, literally, "to build the temple", *ædem facere*.

The most important feature of the rite is freedom. Not only - and no more - the profane freedom, but the initiatory one, which lets the initiate - the man who began to walk the inner path: *in-ire* - to go to the Absolute, *solutus-ab*, that is, loosen from any human contingency. "Liberty" stems from the Sanskrit root *leud*, elevation.

In this new condition there is peace with the Sacred, which is in a heuristic dimension, where knowledge has replaced faith, as faith alone may sometimes be blind and intolerant. This is the peak's experience, of the cosmic consciousness, of the solitude which is seemingly such, because man ideally hugs the One, resting in it.

ON THE ORIGINS OF FREEMASONIC RITUAL

By: Wayne Major

The challenge has been raised over and over concerning Freemasonic rituals that it represents anything ranging from a "distortion" of biblical truth, to outright Satanism. I was prompted to offer this response after seeing one of the latest diatribes on the subject at christianforums.com.

In following the debate on this particular issue, I have seen different theories advanced as to the origins of ritual and the setting in which it arose. The suggestion has been made, and a proper one in my estimation, that for a proper understanding of the rituals of Masonry, we must have a firm grasp of the context from which they arose. As I have sought to keep an open eye and ear for those sources, there is one in particular which I have seen occasionally alluded to, but it seems, never expounded on with a great deal of clarity. Several times I have seen just a sentence or short paragraph acknowledgment that these rituals arise out of medieval "morality plays." I thought it would be a good idea to investigate in greater depth and determine for myself, if possible, the merits of this suggested link. What I found was interesting and informative, and I would like to share some observations.

To begin, I would like to take a look at the morality plays themselves, and the era and social milieu from which they arose. What exactly is a morality play? Morality plays developed from a genre of sacred drama known as mystery plays and miracle plays. The mystery plays were a characterization or re-enactment of key events in scripture. Miracle plays were essentially the same, but were focused more on particular personalities found in scripture, or of historical saints and the miracles wrought in their lives. The morality plays essentially arose and developed from the mystery plays and miracle plays, but there was one particular focus that made them completely different: «Unlike the perspective of the mystery and miracle plays, that of the morality play was individual rather than collective. The morality play (usually called simply a morality) presented religious and ethical concerns from the point of view of the individual Christian, whose main concern was to effect the salvation of his soul. . .»[1]

So it was religious in nature in its beginnings, arising from the dramatizations of the sacred events and scenes of scripture. But a process of secularization had begun even before the morality plays arose as a separate form within the genre. Originally, the cast of characters involved in these plays were the clergy and their congregations. But the Catholic Church frowned on the plays when certain secular elements entered in, and a papal edict issued in 1210 forbade clergy from acting on the public stage.[2] That was merely the first step in further secularization. Increasingly the actors came from townspeople who were not necessarily members of the church, and as a result, supervisory control of the moralities, as they were also called, shifted to the town guilds. With this change, fewer and fewer people understood what was happening onstage in the Latin vernacular, and the Latin was replaced. Eventually other scenes became inserted that were not in the Bible. To increase the dramatic effect of the plays, character and story detail grew in importance. But they still retained their connection to the sacred, and they began to follow the cycle of the Christian Church calendar.

As the interest in them grew, and as they became more refined and enhanced, some definite characteristics began to stand out. A study at Arizona State University notes these characteristics, and makes the bold assertion that we still maintain the same forms in practically every format we have in drama today, be it comedy, or drama, or even the television news:

---

[1] http://ise.uvic.ca/Library/SLTnoframes/drama/moralities.html#fn1
[2] http://encarta.msn.com/encnet/refpages/RefArticle.aspx?refid=761573272

Narrative structure: there's a story that can be told.

Universal and Moral: the story could or does affect many people.

Specific time and place: a specific location and time is involved providing urgency.

Unambiguous: the event either is or can be made to have a cause-effect relationship and is easily understood.

Focus is disorder: something is wrong and there is a solution.

Culturally resonant: the story is something that people can identify with easily.[3]

There are other elements which stand out as well, particularly the struggle of a central character with the forces of good and evil. The characters are generally personifications of some particular virtue or vice, and there are allurements throughout the story that try to persuade the main character to succumb to one or the other. Eventually various representations of the devil gave way to one main character simply known as "Vice," who was the main antagonist who tried to turn the lead character from following his path. By the fifteenth century, the moralities had evolved into a form of secular dinner entertainment, often performed before royal courts. They developed into a briefer, more comic form known as "interludes," after the brief humorous segment included in each play became a standard audience favorite. From this the form even developed into a new breed of political and religious satire. One example of this focus is the play "Mankind":

Within the play there is there is a reference to an imaginary 'Pope Pocket' which is seen as many as a jibe against the Pope's greed. It is also possible that this was a reference to John Poket who was the Prior of Barnwell Abbey, near Cambridge, the area in which 'Mankind' is believed to have originated. John was Prior between 1444 and 1464. Line 514 suggests that Prior had dealings with 'Master Allington of Bottisham', this is seen as a reference to the local

---

[3] http://researchmag.asu.edu/stories/mediaside.html

papal representative of the time. This explains the ironic 'Pope' reference.[4]

There is no doubt that the immortal bard, William Shakespeare, was influenced by the morality plays, as has been attested to by many a Shakespeare historian already. So should it be any surprise that he would be connected with Freemasonry as well?

The Masonic references in the Shakespeare plays are numerous, some fairly obvious and others extremely subtle, but all woven into the text in such a way that they form a natural part of the magical garment. A Freemason is referred to several times and in several ways, as, for instance, referring to the higher degrees, 'a brother of gracious Order, late come from the Sea, in special business from his Holinesse. In Henry V the brethren are referred to as 'the singing masons building roofs of gold'; in King John as 'a worshipful society'; whilst Love's Labour's Lost not only mentions 'profound Solomon' but also the Lodge and a password, suitably disguised:

> *Arm.* I will visit thee at the Lodge.
> *Jaq.* That's hereby.
> *Arm.* I know where it is situate.
> *Jaq.* Lord, how wise you are....
> *Arm.* Come Jaquenetta....[5]

But how may this dramatic form be said to be linked to Freemasonry and/or its development? That depends a great deal on whose format you accept for exactly when Freemasonry developed. The most common understanding is that it arose during this same period, and had its origins in the medieval craft guilds. That would place the development of Freemasonry squarely within the same time frame of the development of the morality plays. The most accurate dating we have for any of the extant morality plays is the

---

[4] http://vzone.virgin.net/numb.world/cathedral.morality.plays2.htm
[5] Peter Dawkins, "Shakespeare and Freemasonry," http://www.sirbacon.org/Dawkinsfrmsnry.htm

play "Mankind," which has been dated by internal evidence in the mention of two coins of the realm, the royal and the angel, which both date from the late 1400's.

With the transition of the mystery plays into the more secular Moralities, one may speculate that the Catholic Church, who denounced them from the very first secular elements they absorbed, would have become increasingly critical of them as they further evolved in that direction. This may certainly be one factor that figured into the historic relationship of animosity of the Catholic Church toward Freemasonry. Ironically, one of the most striking descriptions I found in looking at the connection of the Moralities with Freemasonry, came from a Catholic website:

"The aim of both was religious. In the Miracle play the subject-matter is concerned with Bible narrative, Lives of Saints, the Apocryphal Gospels, and pious legends, a certain historical or traditional foundation underlies the plot, and the object was to teach and enforce truths of the Catholic faith. In the Morality the matter was allegorical rather than historical, and its object was ethical; the cultivation of Christian character. The intention of both Miracle Plays and Moralities, as we have said, was religious; in the one it aimed at faith, the teaching of dogma, in the other morals, the application of Christian doctrine to conduct."[6]

That description is almost a mirror image of much of the current debate, in which Freemasons have made the assertion, as a counter to anti-Masonic claims that Freemasonry is a religion, that it is simply a system designed to teach morals, but morals which are distinctly founded on Christian principles. Of course, the author of that article did not have Freemasonry in mind at all. But there are many writers around who have spotted the connection of Freemasonry with the morality plays:

"Freemasonry is avowedly concerned with morality. Its symbols are interpreted for the candidate in moral terms

---

[6] Kate Mary Warren, "Moralities," *The Catholic Encyclopedia*, Vol. 10, New York: Robert Appleton Company, 1911.

(thus, when the working tools are displayed in the first degree, the candidate is told that 'we apply these tools to our morals') and its ceremonies are effectively morality plays, stressing particular virtues... Freemasonry is an "esoteric art," in that certain aspects of its internal work are not generally revealed to the public. Masons give numerous reasons for this, one of which is that Freemasonry uses an initiatory system of degrees to explore ethical and philosophical issues, and this system is less effective if the observer knows beforehand what will happen..."[7]

There are three initial "degrees" of Freemasonry: (1) Entered Apprentice, (2) Fellow Craft and (3) Master Mason. One works through each degree by taking part in a ritual, essentially a medieval morality Play, in which one plays a role, along with members of the Lodge that one is joining. The setting is Biblical—the building of the Temple of Solomon in Jerusalem—although the stories themselves are not directly from the Bible, and not intended to be necessarily Jewish or Christian in nature. Nothing supernatural happens in these stories. The Temple can be taken to represent the "temple" of the individual human being, that of the human community, or of the entire universe.

As one works through the degrees, one studies the lessons and interprets them for oneself. There are as many ways to interpret the rituals as there are Masons, and no Mason may dictate to any other Mason how he is to interpret them. No particular truths are espoused, but a common structure—speaking symbolically to universal human archetypes—provides for each Mason a means to come to his own answers to life's important questions.[8]

This constant movement of skilled labour from project to project, Lodge to Lodge, country to country, created lines of communication, and an increasing uniformity of stan-

---

[7] Robert Gilbert, "Freemasonry and Esoteric Movements," 1 Mar. 2000, http://www.canonbury.ac.uk/lectures/esoteric.htm
[8] "Freemasonry" http://en.wikipedia.org/wiki/Freemasonry, accessed May 2004.

dards; of modes of recognition and levels of expectation; of "secrets" that were the currency - the coin - of the craft.

Beyond skills, reliable moral and ethical behaviour was expected. Morality plays were developed, sometimes performed in public on construction sites. Were these the source of our modern Degree rituals?[9]

Obviously, there are quite a few people who have answered that question with a well-qualified yes. But within the descriptions provided by these sources, I noticed little details that, in my judgment, bolster the case for the suggested origin of the rituals from the morality plays:

> "The action of the morality play centres on a hero, such as Mankind, whose inherent weaknesses are assaulted by such personified diabolic forces as the Seven Deadly Sins but who may choose redemption and enlist the aid of such figures as the Four Daughters of God (Mercy, Justice, Temperance, and Truth)".[10]

No Mason should have to look twice at this paragraph to see two of the four cardinal virtues, in those four attributes, and a strong emphasis on the other two as well.

Typically, the morality play is a psychomachia, an externalized dramatization of a psychological and spiritual conflict: the battle between the forces of good and evil in the human soul. This interior struggle involves the Christian's attempt to achieve salvation, despite the obstacles and temptations that he encounters as he travels through life, toward death.

In England the moralities dramatized the progress of the Christian's life from innocence to sin, and from sin to repentance and salvation. Among the most widely known of the fifteenth-century moralities are *The Castell of Perseverance*, which features a battle between Virtues and Vices; *Mankind*, which incorporates topical farce; and perhaps the most famous of all the English morality plays, *Everyman* (c.

---

[9] http://www.mastermason.com/pei/faq_essay.asp , accessed May 2004
[10] *Encyclopedia Britannica*, accessed online at
http://www.britannica.com/EBchecked/topic/391805/morality-play

1495), which concerns the Christian's experience of mortality and Judgment.[11]

Think for a moment of the typical anti-Masonic objection to the presence of these themes, suggesting that they reflect "a Masonic plan of salvation." It is one thing to contain these themes as a matter of course within the dramatic form(s) in which the rituals appear; it is quite another to divorce the rituals from their format, strip them of the Christian bearing with which they were conceived, and come up with anything with the least resemblance to truth in whatever understanding is left as a result. Thus the typical anti-Masonic objection to the words in the Fellow Craft degree prologue is totally unfounded when you consider it in comparison with the same themes prevalent in the form from which it derived:

"As you progress through the three degrees, remember also that they are emblematical of the stages of one's life. The Entered Apprentice represents youth, and the attainment of knowledge. The Fellowcraft degree represents manhood, and the application of what has been learned in our youth. And we will see later, that the Master Mason degree represents the man of years, with the wisdom of a lifetime, and the setting sun in his eyes."[12]

The main characters in *Everyman* are God, a Messenger, Death, Everyman, Fellowship, Kindred, Cousin, Goods, Knowledge, Beauty, Strength, and Good Deeds. Everyman is immersed in worldly pleasures when Death summons unexpectedly him. He soon finds that none of his supposedly loyal companions (Fellowship, Kindred, Cousin) will go with him. His treasured Goods also desert him, and at the grave the qualities of the flesh (Beauty, Strength) also fade away. Only Good Deeds stays with him to help him get into Paradise, which is accomplished with the help and guid-

---

[11] *The Morality Play in English Drama*, accessed online at http://www.readprint.com/article-4
[12] Fellow Craft Resource Page, Minneapolis Lodge No. 19, A.F. & A.M., online at http://www.mpls19.org/Fellow_Craft.aspx

ance of Knowledge, by means of Confession and Priesthood.

In other moralities, various manifestations of the forces of Evil (the Seven Deadly Sins, the World, the Flesh, the Devil, Vice) are arrayed against the Christian, who turns for help to the forces of Good (God, His angels, Virtue). The quality of writing in the moralities is uneven, and in many cases the author is unknown. Characterization is also crude and nave, and there is little attempt to portray psychological depth. . . .[13]

Need I point out the obvious virtues, and the themes, that are characteristic of the rituals of Freemasonry? I would think most Masons would recognize the similarities on sight.

The connection of Masonic ritual to a dramatic form of its time raises questions that must of necessity be raised, whether speaking of Masonic ritual, or of Scripture, or of any other literary work which comes down to us from a time and culture very different from our own: What were the forms? What was the influence on both structure and content? To what degree did these affect the writing in question? How does this influence affect the way we approach interpretation and understanding? To what degree does it alter what we have already come to believe and accept?

In answering these questions, the measure to which we acknowledge and allow the influence of a very specific literary genre and form, will greatly influence our understanding of the content. In this case, my own assessment is, that it is very clear there was significant influence from the morality plays in the style and presentation of these ritual enactments, enough to make it impossible to ignore the significance of allegorical interpretation of their content, and of the characters represented.

---

[13] *The Morality Play in English Drama.*

THE INITIATE'S WORK

By: Giuseppe Vinci

Citing the Poet, we could say that *midway on the journey of our life*[1] the need of the inner improvement led us to knock at the door of the temple. We however recognize – at least we ought to – that we are a finite, limited, imperfect entity, subject to continuous change; fleeting, always in the reign of the dualism, between good and evil, nice and ugly, right and wrong and so on forever. The human condition wriggles continuously between the finite and the infinite. Being finite we long for the infinite, the absolute, the perfection.

The fight of the contraries is not, however, a mere philosophical idea. The self-conscious man is aware that this hard struggle has to be fought on the field of his own life, which is impregnated with difficulties and successes, suffering and happiness, mistakes and glory, hate and love.

Along this path, knowledge *(jñana)* is the instrument which helps to approach the perfection. The knowledge we are speaking about, however, is that which conducts us toward the truth, it is not erudition, *viz.* that which is obtained by reading books or studying either at any school or even at any university. This latter can be of some help for us, but it is quite unnecessary to gain a superior level of knowledge *(paravidya)*.

Initiates search after the knowledge of the Self *(vidyaa)*, as from the individual one *(atman)* to the universal one *(paramaatman)*.

In the bookshops man can find a lot of papers dealing with initiatory stories, but this is merely initiatory education and not initiation itself. Education, as it is commonly intended in the West, could even remove an individual from the true spirit of the initiation. Let us recall the words of Plato, written in the Apology: *that God only is wise; and by*

---

[1] Dante, *The Comedy,* Inf. I, 1

his answer he intends to show that the wisdom of men is worth little or nothing...[2]

The true initiatory experience is the provisions to take an inner journey in order to know oneself, to conquer the truth, to walk along the path of the inner improvement, thus getting full mastery and self-knowledge.

The initiatory experience allows us to experiment the truth; the essence and the acquaintance that are so gained are, above all, cathartic acquaintance, the door to the deep transformation of the conscience. To be masters *(guru – acarya)*, therefore, does not mean to have a pedantic book learning. To be masters means to realize a status of conscience, a dignity that no mental and intellectual erudition will ever be able to give. The initiatory acquaintance is transmitted from "ear to mouth", from master to disciple *(guruparamparam)*, through a complex ritualistic and symbolic apparatus, that it is handed on for an immemorial time and constitutes the initiatory tradition. Which is the place where the initiates can improve their instruments that are necessary to transmute themselves and eventually get the supreme liberation *(moksa)*.

The primary work, or better, the primary duty to enter into the temple of the truth consists in being conscious of one's own flaws and to correct them. This work is like an unceasing struggle on the field of our being, in order to search after and to rectify it. We have to clear the field from its historical enemies: the ego and the ambition, the presumption and the pride, the desires and the vanity, old always alive sons of the ignorance: *in us a God lives that can only speak in absence of vanity, of pride, of poor profane interests; in presence of heart's purity.*

The initiatory work can be fruitful if it is done with engagement and dedication, love and devotion *(bhakti)* towards our Being, the inner Self, that God that remains silent since it is wrapped in the darkness of the ignorance *(avidya)*, in the veil of the prejudgment and the presump-

---

[2] Plato, *Apology*

tion, in the mantle of the attachments, of the illusions *(maya)* that weight down, slow down and often prevent the way towards the light. The realization begins to give its yields progressively, while man is working on his own transformation, facing the more difficult fight that the man has never fought: that against his passions, against his conflict *ego*.

A very hard work, to be done in silence and secrecy, within our inner. The attachments of the profane life, the desire of money, the ambitions and the prejudices must be kept under strict control and possibly rejected during the journey.

The charity is useless to transmute oneself. It demagogically cleans our conscience, but has no effect on the inner transformation. Charity and other pious actions is the natural by-product of the man who realized himself, that is free from the neuroses, that has gone beyond the appearances. Who has caught self-conscience he actually works for his transmutation, in total respect of the Tradition; he will then be brought beyond the time and the space, till to the Supreme Knowledge.

To know is therefore to be. This is the identity's principle of the initiatory realization. Man has to directly experiment this assumption. By means of a constant self-discipline *(sadhana),* this knowledge will become a life style, a true habit rather than a mere appearance.

In their cultural patrimony, any and all traditions represent the three phases of the realization. Essentially, they consist in:

1. A process of descent into the deepest inner, to purify oneself;
2. A subsequent process of assimilation in which man learns how to conform to the traditional teachings; the individual conscience is thus expanded and is going to merge into the universal one;
3. The full identification with the Truth.

The being, totally free *(ivan-mukta),* is now the shining sun where there are no differences between light, fire and burning matter: he is the pure Self. Man becomes what he thinks, affirms *Maitry Upanishad.*

Even if the initiation is practiced in a community, it is nevertheless a unique, ineffable experience. Man has to live it directly, in person. Nobody could rationally describe it, even by approximate words. As said Plato, nobody can be our substitute for the solution of the *Eternal Mystery.*

THE INITIATIC SECRET

By: R. Theron Dunn

There are many secrets in the world in which we live, which holds true in Freemasonry. The initiatic secret, however, is a peculiar one. The secret is the key concept of any initiatory society, being quite different from any other kind of secret which can be encountered in every organization.

The word "secret" stems from Latin *se-cernere*, to set apart and aside at the same time; "initiatic" – and also "initiatory, initiate" – derives from the Latin verb *in-ire*, to go into, in depth. The expression, therefore, alludes to something which a man comes across walking the inner path and then grasps in his deepest soul. The true secrets of Freemasonry are personal, and are different for every man, and for this reason, the secret is truly ineffable and cannot be communicated, even willingly.

This is why Br. René Guénon wrote: *In fact this secret is of such a nature that words cannot express it* and why, Br. Giovanni Giacomo Casanova wrote:

Those who become Freemasons only for the sake of finding out the secret of the order, run a very great risk of growing old under the trowel without ever realizing their purpose. Yet there is a secret, but it is so inviolable that it has never been confided or whispered to anyone. Those who stop at the outward crust of things imagine that the secret consists in words, in signs, or that the main point of it is to be found only in reaching the highest degree. This is a mistaken view: the man who guesses the secret of Freemasonry, and to know it you must guess it, reaches that point only through long attendance in the lodges, through deep thinking, comparison, and deduction.

He would not trust that secret to his best friend in Freemasonry, because he is aware that if his friend has not found it out, he could not make any use of it after it had been whispered in his ear. No, he keeps his peace, and the secret remains a secret.[1]

It can seem contradictory to hold out that Freemasonry can teach the secrets, while at the same time noting that we cannot communicate them. This is part of the mystery of the initiatic method, one that uses rites and symbols to suggest and lead, rather than express, in the ordinary sense of the word.

"Properly speaking, what is transmitted by initiation is not the secret itself, since this is incommunicable, but the spiritual influence that the rites vehicle and that makes possible the interior work by means of which, with the symbols as base and support, each one will attain that secret and penetrate it more or less completely, more or less profoundly, according to the measure of his own possibilities of comprehension and realization."[2]

The initiatic secret is a method of spiritual improvement, which stems from a hard inner work aimed to transform the initiate, that is to make him go beyond his present form in order to achieve a new one: it refuses religious dogmas and pushes initiates toward a perfection's status, which, even if unattained, nevertheless will be considered a rule for their actions.

Freemasonry is an initiatic society, one whose rituals and mystic rites are as much about wakening the inner spiritual man as about improving the moral, material man. Undertaken in the proper mindset, with a man properly prepared, both in his mind and in his heart, the ritual of Freemasonry will set him on the first step to a spiritual awakening.

This spiritual awakening is, after all, what the initiatic experience is all about. We are told in the ritual, ask and it shall be given, seek and you will find, knock, and the door

---

[1] Giovanni Giacomo Casanova, *Memoirs*, Volume 2°, Paris, p. 33
[2] R. Guénon, "The initiatic secret", in *Perspectives on Inititiation*, Sophia Perennis, p. 85

will be opened to you. This is as plain and open as initiatory rites get for a man.

Yet, it is up to the man to seek. The degrees only prepare a man, open his eyes so he can see the door. It is up to the candidate to walk the path. Since the secrets of Freemasonry cannot be communicated, the man must undertake the search and do the work. Nothing worth having comes easily.

A further consequence is that such a secret cannot be betrayed, because profanes are outside the initiatory world so void of any means – rites and symbols – to do any inner work.

Freemasonry is not a secret society, even if it has a "closed" character. This does not hinge upon a reason of prudence – even if in the past times persecutions justified it – but rather to avoid the danger of degeneration, by admitting profanes who are not fully qualified to grasp the secret. These men will remain profanes with the apron, and soon or later they will "waste the chain", because they are reluctant to walk the inner path.

"As for the fact that these organizations are 'closed', that is, that they do not admit everyone indiscriminately, this is explained simply by the first condition of initiation described above, the necessity of possessing certain particular 'qualifications' lacking which no real benefit can be derived from attachment to such an organization. Moreover, when an initiatic organization becomes too 'open' and insufficiently strict in this respect, it runs the risk of degenerating through the incomprehension of those whom it thus thoughtlessly admits, who, especially when they become the majority, do not fail to introduce all sorts of profane opinions and to divert its activity toward goals that have nothing in common with the initiatic domain, as one sees only too often in what still remains of this kind of organization in the Western world today."[3]

---

[3] R. Guénon, *ibidem*, p.86

Mediocre minds despise and hate what they cannot understand.

Man has not to confuse the initiatic secret with the prohibition to reveal grips, tokens and signs. They cannot be disclosed for two reasons. The first consists in that, that they are symbols like any other and therefore are to be meditated and internalized. They are means to elaborate the initiatic secret and therefore man has to treat them with due reverence and seriousness.

The second reason is the silence's pedagogic role. The 'discipline of the secret' constitutes a sort of 'training' or exercise that is part of the method of these organizations—and this can be seen in a way as an attenuated and restricted form of the 'discipline of silence' that was used in certain ancient esoteric schools, particularly among the Pythagoreans. *Disciplina secreti* or *disciplina arcani*, as it was also called in the Church of the first centuries, something that certain enemies of the 'secret' seem to forget; but it should be noted that in Latin the word *disciplina* usually signifies 'teaching',[4] which is its etymological meaning, and even, by derivation, 'science' or 'doctrine'.

To keep a secret thus enhances character.

---

[4] From Latin *discere*, to learn. Discipline is the means to learn

THE SYMBOL

By: Nicola Grenci

In Ancient Greek, the word "symbol" stood for means of control or means of recognition, made by breaking an object into two irregular parts, in such a way the owners of the parts could recognise each other by putting the two together again. Taken separately, one of the pieces also represents its owner. The symbol, in fact, hides deeper meanings. The mystic Ugo di San Vittore describes symbols as "the use of the visible, to show the invisible".

One's comprehension of a symbol is strictly related to the knowledge one has already acquired. It is plain that the development of a symbolic imagination never ends; we can find symbols even where no human reasoning has ever seen one before.

While the profane world communicates by words, initiates communicate by symbolism. Traditional symbols, in fact, join the material and spiritual worlds through a synthesis grounded on intuitive knowledge (pure transcendent intellect). The origin of this intuitive knowledge is not in the mind (because it transcends the mind) but rather in the "centre" of the individual (the "centre-hearth" of certain traditions), where resides the divine light from which we originate.

This is possible because a traditional symbol is part of the sacred, although it does not reveal it.

It is a duty of the initiate to reveal the living and operating reality, the reality of the sacred which the symbol frames, because it stimulates the consciousness through the creative imagination. However, this is essentially an acknowledgment, an increased awareness of the Truth—in other words, *Gnòsis*.

Symbols have at various times represented the only way to preserve and to hand down memory and knowledge. In order to understand Masonic symbols, we must release certain structures of the profane culture which force us to attribute to the symbol just one meaning, which eventually transforms the symbol into a code. The richness of the initiate's inner journey is limited only by the breadth of possibilities connected to it.

As Di Bernardo wrote:

In Freemasonry the symbol expresses just one secret: the initiatory secret. There is just one initiation, in which one senses oneself to be part of the ideal chain of the Fraternity. He who is unable to understand this will always find himself to be a profane who has entered the Masonic Temple by chance, who observes familiar objects, like the square, the compasses, the gavel... without being able to understand their real symbolic meaning.

The symbols that surround us in the temple have progressively achieved so much potentiality that one can read and interpret them in many different ways.

It is also true that through them (and even more through the rituals) we will become able to find the way to look for "the Truth".

Those who deny that symbols carry any kind of deeper meaning for the most part probably do not have the psychological capacity to think in symbolic terms, to detach themselves from everyday life in order to confront and begin the symbolic work which is peculiar to his community

Anything can be a symbol, if we that is all we want. Symbols refer to physical reality only indirectly, but nevertheless they directly underline a mental, imagined reality comprising meanings and sense.

Ernst Cassier stated that man is a symbolic animal. Following a hermetic concept, he is "an incarnation of cosmic functions", or, because he is placed at the centre of creation, he is considered the *Universal Symbol*.

We can say that we have not only visual symbols, but auditory ones as well.

Now I would like you to think about one of our rituals: it is constituted by a group of visual symbols (objects which are in the temple, our aprons). Words and gestures are however symbols, too. We can say that they are symbols involving action.

The interpretation of symbols, then, is up to the intelligence and the sensitivity of each one of us, through an inner quest which leads us to find our microcosm within.

This interpretation should not have a dogmatic character, and can assume therefore different meanings without experiencing contradictions; on the contrary, it is self-completing.

We can in fact affirm that symbols cannot be completely disclosed, explained and rationalised, because each attempt in such direction will deprive them of their magical dimension. Furthermore, we can state that symbols promote free thought, contrary to all religious and political dogmas.

As our Bro. Rocco Ritorto wrote, "ritualism and symbolism are the means to drive the Mason to that light which frees him from superstition, fanaticism, and dogmatism, allowing him to enrich his Ego with knowledge; without this, any path of truth and spiritual, moral, and intellectual growth is vain".

The experiential entry by means of symbols onto an inner path connected with the rituality of the temple allows the initiate to proceed towards the highest of journeys, the path of "know thyself".

I conclude with a quote of Bachofen:

> *It is in the graves that the symbol has been created…*
> *Thoughts, feelings, dumb prayers*
> *Evoked by the aspect of the tomb*
> *Could not be expressed by words;*
> *Just the symbol, because of its immutable silence,*
> *Can enable one to feel them.*

THE SYMBOL AND ITS FUNCTION

By: *Anonym*[1]

The word "symbol" stems from the Greek *symballéin*, to put together, to assemble, to unify. It was a coin, or a ring or something else, which man broke into two pieces, so that, by joining them, their holders could recognize themselves.

So doing man synthesizes. At a traditional level, and also by definition, any synthesis starts from 'principles', that is, from the inner and, therefore, the esoteric human side.

Traditional symbols unite the matter to the spirit by a synthetic proceeding which is grounded on intuition (the pure transcendent intellect), the siege of which is not in the mind, since this is transcended by it, but in the heart, in the center of any human being, where man finds the divine spark which is within as from the Origin.

This happens for traditional symbols share the sacred and re-veal it, that is, veil it once again. It is [the] iniates' task to unveil the sacred's living reality which is hidden by the symbol for it urges the conscience to open itself by the creative imagination. This process consists in realizing the truth; it is, therefore, Gnosis.

The symbol is synthetic and universal, its language can be always understood anywhere. It joins the particular to the universal, thus taking men back to the One.

The Word, about which John speaks in his gospel and on which Freemasons lay square and compasses, is the first symbol which contains all the other ones, as well as any manifestation which derives from it.

This symbol is actually a vibration, as well as the monosyllable OM, which is a name of Logos. "By this word we begin to pray", a Lama said to Ossendowsky. «Surprisingly, man finds this word (OM) also in the ancient Christian symbolism, where, among other symbols of Christ, man comes across one word which was later Christianized into an ab-

---
[1]Translation of Giovanni Lombardo

breviation of Mary, but was firstly considered a means to join the extreme letters of the Greek alphabet, *alpha* and *omega*, so to signify that the Word is, at the same time, principle and end of everything. Actually, it is even more complete, because it means principle, middle and end. Man can break up it as AVM, that is the three Latin letters which match the three elements which constitute the monosyllable OM (in Sanskrit the vowel "o" is made up by "a" and "u")».[2]

The traditional language is symbolic and therefore synthetic, while that of the profane world is analytic: the former unifies, the latter separates. *Syn-bolon* and *dia-bolon: deus inversus est dæmon,* the devil is an inverted God. Profanity speaks a diabolic language, the same confused language which Dante hears at Inferno: "Strange utterances, horrible pronouncements".[3] When Jesus asks the Devil for his name, he answers: "My name is Legion, for we are many".[4]

The Truth descends from above to below by the symbol's conciseness while man conversely ascends, availing himself of the symbol, to higher and more comprehensive laws. We could say that Truth goes toward a man to the extent he goes toward Truth. Popular wisdom expressed the idea by the proverb "God helps them that help themselves".

The symbol's function consists in joining the particular to the universal, thus expressing what cannot be otherwise expressed. Therefore Olympiodorus said that the symbols' power is far greater than anything else.

If a qualified man assimilates the symbol, then he becomes the symbol itself, realizing and enhancing the truth which is hidden in it. This is its function: to lift a man to the Truth, to let him become aware of it and make himself similar to it, *id est* to assimilate it.

---

[2] *Il Re del Mondo*, p. 31, footnote 1. [Romans read V as "v" or "u", as the case may be. ED]
[3] *Inf.* III, 25
[4] *Mark* 5, 9

THE ASHLAR UNFOLDED

By: John S. Nagy

Above all, stone is. It always remains itself, and exists of itself; ... Rock shows him [mankind] something that transcends the precariousness of his humanity; an absolute mode of being. Its strength, its motionlessness, its size and its strange outlines are none of them human; they indicate the presence of something that fascinates, terrifies, attracts and threatens, all at once. In its grandeur, its hardness, its shape and its colour, man is faced with a reality and a force that belong to some world other than the profane world of which he is himself a part.
(Mircea Eliade, *Patterns in comparative religion*, chap. 6)

If you've heard the word "Ashlar" used in Freemasonry, it's because Masons work in Stone and Stone Work is a dominant  Theme. The Words "Stone" and "Ashlar" are literal in their reference but figurative in any application in Masonic Work. The Stone that any Mason works is the Stone of a Mason's Self. Worked Stone, as in "a Stone that is dressed in some fashion," is called "Ashlar." To understand more fully the reasons why the word "Stone" and "Ashlar" are used in Masonry though one must look into some of the history behind their references.

The use of the word "Stone" specifically derives from the understanding that Human Beings are a mix of both Spirit and Flesh. Reading this, one might at once raise a voice in protest by saying, "What do these have to do with Stone, which is neither Spirit nor Flesh?" The reasons may not be clear or obvious at first glance until further connections are uncovered. Let's explore these connections further.

The spiritual aspect of our Being, is classically referred to as "The Father/Source"; the physical aspect of our Being, is classically referred to as "The Son." When these two aspects are put forth using Hebrew words, "Father" is written as "AB" and it means "the Strength of the House"; "Son" is written as "BN" and it means "To Continue the House."

Stone plays into this in a specific manner. By melding the Hebrew words for Father and Son or AB-BN, the Hebrew word for Stone "ABN" is created. When this word is used as a verb, ABN means, "Build"; when it is used as a noun, it means "Stone." In that melding of the Spirit and Flesh, called humankind, "Built-Stone" is created. *Above all, Masonry is the Craft of Working with this Built-Stone.*

If you take a good look at the majority of Stone that exists in our world today, and all that has ever existed, you can easily see that most of it is locked up in earth. Further survey tells you immediately that most Stone is created "captured" by the surrounding aggregate and it is not free to do anything other than merely exist in that bound up state.

Some of this Stone though is released from the ground, which once held it firmly. This freed up Stone is just that, merely "freed up" and hence is quite appropriately called "Freestone." Freestone is not Ashlar though. To become Ashlar, Freestone must be worked or dressed in some manner or form. Until it is, it is merely free.

After it is released from the ground and freed from the binds that held it in place, only Freestone with good character will be selected for the Builder's use.

Initially, Freestone that is Worked and roughly squared at the quarry is referred to as "Bastard Ashlar." It has yet to be moved for use. It is however, further examined at this point to determine if it has the qualities that would be useful to the Builder. If it has detrimental flaws, character traits that show it to be missing elements that would cause failure should it be further worked and then united with other Stones, the Builder will reject it. If it shows itself to be without these flaws and has good prospects for becoming a Perfect Ashlar, then the Builder may choose to remove it from the quarry for use.

Once the Freestone is moved from the quarry for use though, this dressed Stone is then referred to "Rough Ashlar." It is called such because it was chosen for the Builder's use but it has yet to be shaped and finished. Rough Ashlar is Stone in an untutored, unpolished and unrefined state.

Rough Ashlars are the state in which Future Masons arrive at and enter into Masonry. Candidates, in the Rough Ashlar state, have already been properly characterized as individuals whom are of high regard, well vouched for, of legal age, and a host of other considerations, depending on the Masonic Order of choice.

With entry into a Masonic Order, the Rough Ashlar, now Entered Apprentice, is introduced to a variety of Working tools during the Entered Apprentice Degree that are designed to help him in his further Stone Work. Since the Work to be done is to one's own Stone, it's up to the Entered Apprentice to learn how to use the Tools of the Craft well. For this to occur, other Stones called "Fellow Craft Masons" and "Master Masons" are available to assist in the Entered Apprentice's Stone Work.

As Rough Ashlar is Worked and is hammer-dressed, it is called a "Common-Ashlar." As Masonic Work proceeds on the Stone that is the Rough Ashlar or Entered Apprentice, it is eventually crafted into a "Perfect Ashlar."

Please note that the use of the word "perfect," and all the Masonic variations in its use when referring to Ashlars, does not denote "flawlessness." This assumption that "flawlessness" means "perfection" is a dangerous one that will lead the best of intended Masons down a road of never being of any great use to the Builder. Masons believing that they are Working toward flawlessness are misguided. They operate with a false belief. When Freestone is selected by the Builder for Work *to be done upon it, it is selected because it is already seen to be without flaws that would prevent it from being used.*

Let's stress these last points once again: Perfection in working Ashlar refers to the "maturing" and bringing it to the state in which it has use for the Builder. In other words, *the Perfect Ashlar shows no flaw that would prevent it from being used before it is Perfected and is called "Perfect" only when it has reached a point when it has use to the Builder.*

There are also differences in the meaning of "Ashlar" when it comes to Masonry and actual stone working. In Masonry, useful Stones are considered "Perfect Ashlars"; these Stones have all six faces cut at right angles so they can be joined smoothly to other Perfect Ashlars. In actual stone working practice though, useful stones are considered "ashlars"; these stones are cut square only on the sides intended to adjoin to other ashlars, no matter whether non-adjoining faces are dressed or not.

To assist a Mason in transforming toward usefulness, more tools are introduced to the Entered Apprentice during the Fellow Craft Degree. Once this Degree concludes, the Entered Apprentice is then a Fellow Craft Mason and is expected to Prefect the Rough Ashlar with those Working Tools. To do this Work though, it is important for the Fellow Craft to understand that, just in the case of the Entered Apprentice Stone Work, nothing is added to the Stone being Worked. A Worked Stone is only to have things removed that are not conducive to a Perfected state.

With skilled use of the given Masonic Working Tools, the Stone is thus transformed from its Rough state to its Perfect state. Only after "what is not needed" has been removed does the Worked Stone become useful to the Builder. This Perfected Stone, now called the "Perfect Ashlar," is a Stone suitable for use in the Building of a "house, not made with hands, eternal in the heavens." Stone in this state is well educated, polished and refined. The Masonic Work on the Stone itself is complete.

Yet, it is also premature to believe that all Masonic Work is completed at this stage. It has not. While one might conclude that the Masonic Work on one's Stone ends after Perfecting the Ashlar, this conclusion is misleading. There is further Work to be done and this Work requires other Perfect Ashlars to commence. More specifically, Perfect Ashlars that have been Raise and Cemented into one unified Structure must be involved. These are the Stones called "Master Masons." Master Masons are those Perfect Ashlars whose Stone Work continues with the unified efforts of other Perfect Ashlars. Exploring a little background on this reveals how this occurs.

In Ancient Masonic Ritual, there is mention of a special Stone called the "Perpend Ashlar" or "Bond Stone." It's a Building term used by Stonemasons to describe Perfect Ashlars used to connect the Inner and Outer layers of walls that create Buildings. Stone walls are usually built with two layers of Perfect Ashlar, an inner and an outer, and may or may not have rubble sandwiched between them. Either way, these two walls require connecter Stones to stabilize the Structure thus Built. Perpend Stones are those Stones whose lengths allow them to extend from the outside of the outer wall to the inside of the inner wall thus showing their smooth faces on the construct's inner and outer surfaces. All the Stones used in the construct are Raised into position, properly aligned and placed.

Once placed, these Stones are then joined together as one unified interlocking mass. Unification is done using Cement (a.k.a. "Brotherly Love"), spread with yet another working tool, to allow these unified structures to be created. The amount of Cement required is directly proportional to the roughness of the finish. Rougher finishes require the most amount of Cement; smoother finishes require far less Cement to unify a Structure. The former does not allow for the closeness that the latter does by default.

Whether used as a Perpend or Perfect Ashlar in any construct, both Stone types use all the tools of the Craft to assure that what is Built has Integrity. A single Stone lacking Integrity jeopardizes anything that is Built.

When Perfect Ashlars are Raised into position, placed in proper alignment with others and cemented together with others, they create Buildings that enable all to contribute best to each other's welfare.

From the ground comes the Stone, freed from that which binds and prevents its perfection and contribution. Thus selected, Stone is crafted, eventually matured and bound in Brotherly love to contribute to the welfare of all.

THE SILENCE OF THE INITIATE

By: Enrico Franceschetti

Preamble

Dearest Brethren,

The subject I am going to introduce tonight with your brotherly support, regards an aspect (or rather a preamble) of our initiatory work, today so difficult to pursue because we are so confused by the deafening daily life.

Before getting to the heart of the matter, though, we must make two preliminary considerations.

The first one concerns the most remarkable characteristic of the western tradition and experience of thought and method; it diverges considerably from the most known (in the profane world) 'oriental tradition'.[1]

In the latter the first element that appears to the western observer is the contemplating-passive disposition that the student or the researcher takes whilst waiting for an illumination. It can be resumed in the sentence: "in one instant a man becomes a perfect Buddha". Man's consciousness is immersed in a meditation that annuls individuality and conscience of self, from the Samsara to the Nirvana.[2]

The western tradition is the result of different environmental and historical experiences and therefore it applies methods of an active nature; it means that in them the in-

---

[1] Oriental mysticism has been made famous because it has been made banal; its most spectacular aspects (levitation, ability to stop the heartbeat) have been given relevance. It is less known, on the other hand, what is the fundament of that tradition, which is the authentic aspiration to knowledge even when pursued through methods different from the ones we are used to.

[2] From the pain of continuous birth and death to the eternal peace. The continuation of individual existence in any form, even as a god, means pain, because existence means to become and to become is the shadow of being, a renewed bribe, a never satisfied desire, an implacable pain. The peace is in the unconscious dissolution in the colorless light where all things are originated and that, without us knowing it, shines in us.

struments of thought of the initiate must be refined to allow an introspection that exalts our consciousness; this will lead to superior states of conscience-knowledge. When we talk about 'superior states of conscience' we mean as Guénon says: "not super-individual states, but to lead the being beyond any conditioned state".

The second necessary consideration remarks the environment where our initiatory work is faced and accomplished.

In the reality of our days the Brother Mason is a man who, in a sense, leads a double inner life. One of them is the citizen, father and husband, fully integrated in the mechanisms of profane life and tied to it in order to contribute properly to the development of human society. The other life is the initiate's, as a man in search of the meanings of the symbol and a traveler in the maze of himself.

The specific task of the Brother Mason is to make these two aspects of his existence live together; he wouldn't be a Brother if he wasn't committed to the perfection of Man and of the human Family, if he wasn't productively present in his society.[3] He is not a distant hermit, neither an abstract observer; he is at the same time Initiate Man «AND» Civil Man. This means that it is necessary to harmonize the great work of refinement of one's inner stone with the life that we call profane; the latter must represent to the outside the Sacred Temple inside each of us.

Well, then, how to prepare heart and soul to refine one's consciousness? How to obtain the 'moral strength' that allows him to fight against adversities and to be an Initiate Brother Mason?

Reaching ... the Silence.

---

[3] The presence of the Brother Mason in the civil society must be intended as presence in itself and not coordinated intervention. The transparency of his Inner Temple will affect whoever is around him and will produce the elevation and the improvement mentioned in the Old Charges.

The Beginning

The word initiation, from *initium*, means 'access' or 'start' and it refers to a 'second birth' (or we could say a 'second start'). Such 're-generation' opens to the being the doors of a world other than the world where the activity occurs in the normal corporeal way; it leads him to the restoration in himself of the 'primordial status' which is fullness and perfection of human individuality.

The primordial status, though, is nothing but the quiet status of the new creation, of the *tabula rasa* on which we can write the words of knowledge, on which we can erect the first bricks of the Sacred Temple.[4]

From the creation of a new status of conscience is derived the first Silence induced by the lack of notions and information. In this sense the Brother just initiated faces the moment of the first exploration of the Sacral Vacuum created around him.

This vacuum, not to be confused with the Mystical Nothing[5] of the Zen tradition, is a 'fertile' vacuum, a direct consequence of the 're-creation' occurred; it becomes an immediate preamble to the following step of understanding and analysis of the new space which the initiate is in.[6]

We must be Silent to get – essentially, that is *in essence* - in touch with the deepest Self.

---

[4] Doctrinal knowledge is necessary to the initiate. Its theoretical understanding is a prerequisite to any 'realization' and it doesn't have anything to do with whatever is exterior education or profane 'knowledge'. Indeed, the latter can be an obstacle rather than a help.

[5] The following short Zen tale explains this concept: "the Master Joshu asked one of his disciples one day: - *What are you?* – the disciple answered: - *I'm in meditation, in the status of Nothing and therefore I'm nothing* – the Master Joshu then told him: - *you must abandon the thought of being nothing, you must abandon your thoughts!*"

[6] Virtual initiation, like the transmission of 'light', is in a certain sense suffered by the candidate, because it is a conveyance and a transmission of a spiritual influence from a regular traditional organization. It obtains a true 'new creation' that upsets the inner balance of the initiating, bringing new Light to him.

Only Silence allows us to perceive the apparently unperceivable sound, the faint noise in the background that, at this stage, is the vibration[7] of one's own being.[8]

Silence leads to the reflection on one's own inner status, it allows one to focus the attention on what was overwhelmed by the noise of a previous unconscious existence and therefore it was kept unsaid; or it might have being unheard because it was covered by noises of every kind.

During the ceremony of initiation to the First Degree some 'journeys' are imposed to the profane. In this process he is accompanied by noises which are strong, invasive and obsessing at first and then they slowly become weak and discreet. Let's remember the words that the Worshipful Master says in this occasion: «Profane, the symbolic journey you've carried out is the picture of human life. The noise you heard reminds us of the passion that moves it; the obstacles you've faced are the difficulties that man faces and he can win or overcome only by acquiring the moral strength that allows him to fight adversities...»

This status so well described precedes the *traditio* of Light; it changes and turns during the Rite, when the initiation's conferrer becomes the proper 'transmitter' and 're-creator'; he acts not as an individual but as a link of a 'chain' whose starting point is outside and beyond humankind.

This new status is produced by the advent of Light; the Apprentice must analyze and take it in (that is *to take it in himself*, make it his own) from his new and next point of view.

The violent contrast experienced during this difficult stage and the sudden change from racketing noise to deep silence can confuse the man who feels it; sometimes it can be quite disconcerting. In actual fact the Apprentice must

---

[7] Many scholars have dealt with the analogies between Vibration-Sound-Light, taking the analogy as far as between Creation and sound.

[8] A great character of Italian theater, Edoardo De Filippo, invited to listen to the 'Voices inside'.

undergo a period of 'material silence' in the Masonic Temple; this will give him the time to mature the new rule, to absorb the *choc* induced by the occurring of such apparently antithetical experiences.

The Development

Once the initiate has accomplished the first and most urgent work, once he's explored and 'recognized' (known again) the space around him, he will turn his eyes further beyond and he will start the work of 're-creation' of the world.

Now the Silence expresses the Time of the advent of the Logos, of the waiting for the Word. In the Silence the Sound will appear.

In India the sound of Krishna's flute originates the world by magic. Pre-Hellenistic divinities play the lyre with the same meaning. Many traditional doctrines consider the sound as the first created thing that originated all the other things, such as light, air and fire.

J. R. R. Tolkien[9] in his *Silmarillion* derives the birth of the world from the Gods' singing; even disharmony which creates Evil is included in the glory and the great mechanism of the creation.

All this must be 'caught on' by the initiate, in order for him to be part of his conscience and to learn how to talk.

It is very interesting to study the definition of phonetic symbolism in some mithraic rituals as it was derived from the Egyptian tradition, mentioned in the *Book of Dead:* «... the word, which is basically an acoustic phenomenon, has more value as a sound than as an expression of ideas, because the sound contained in it and emanated by it is in certain vibrations the modulation of the cosmic breath;[10] to

---

[9] Tolkien is a famous English writer born on the 3rd January 1892 in South Africa. He wrote many fantastic sagas that share a unique vision of an imaginary world; their reading has many levels. We can find in them clear and deep esoteric references.

[10] The value of sound for all traditions is decisive. It is the manifestation of the first and most elementary duality deriving from the creation

pronounce 'correctly' a word and synchronize it, so to speak, with the different rhythms of the cosmos, means to give it back its elemental power». This belief in the phonetic power itself led Gnostics and the followers of Mithra[11] to include parts without any literal meaning in their verses and ritual speeches. The aim was to originate a kind of symbolical music that could act only thanks to the power of the phonetic meaning.

The *Om (Aum)* of Tibetans concentrates the whole universal essence (*A*, principle; *U*, transition; *M*, end, deep sleep). In other words this is the Word that can be heard only if we can be Silent, necessary prerequisite for inner search and authentic knowledge and understanding.

Unfortunately today the Word has lost its sense and with it the Word of God. Since the sense of the Word is lost or misunderstood, profane man tends to do the same with Silence, feeling it like a status to run away from, like an expression of his anguish, unsaid fears and inability to 'see'.

The Initiate Brother has undergone 'a new start', has started to move his first steps, has 'recognized' the Sacred Vacuum surrounded by the Silence generating the Sound; he has perceived the Cosmic Sound as an element that starts Life. Can he walk along the streets of the new world[12]

(Emptiness = Silence = Darkness / Life = Sound = Light). It permeates and expresses the idea of Life itself, of Cosmos as a sensitive manifestation of the environment where Life shows itself. Therefore the vibration induced by sounds is the 'bearing harmonics' of Life itself; the word is a coded organization of sounds and ends up by representing meanings, re-calling sensations that go beyond the mere linguistic conventions.

[11] Ancient deity of the Iranian and Persian religion. He was then identified with the Sun and Apollo and it became the center of a mysterial cult; the main Mithra's exploit was the killing of the Cosmic Bull that, by dying, originates life. Mithraic mysteries were celebrated in underground sanctuaries (mitrei) and ended with a sacred banquet.

[12] Juan Cirliot in his *Dictionary of Symbols* identifies it as 'The Domain where a stage of the existence develops... Twenty-first arcane of the Tarots, it corresponds to the complex of union of the manifested, which is the space world as a reflection of a permanent creative activity'.

created in himself without being a victim of contradictions, contractions and deformities deriving by the contrast between the ever-present profane noise and the clear white received Light?

Once again the answer is... in the Silence.

The Rite, the Instrument, the Guardian

Once again Silence has the role of clarifying and catalyzing in the soul of the Initiate; only the latter knows how to obtain it and to make it a meek instrument in his hands, a fertile preamble and a safe comfort.

There's more.

In the 're-creation' of the Initiation the profane experiences for the first time the Silence, as we said. Therefore the Silence as a first manifestation of a new creation constitutes the intimate ritual of the Brother Mason.

Every rite symbolizes and reproduces creation in its essence. For this reason rites are connected with ornaments and symbols whose intimate identity with the rite is such that they are part of it. The slowness in the ritual moves in ceremonies is similar to the rhythms of astral movements; on the other hand all rites are meetings, confluences of forces and ordinations, concentrations of energies. Its meaning and its power is derived by the accumulation and the combination of the concentrated powers.

The rite as a common character to all traditional institutions of every order, both exoterical and esoterical, has always the purpose of putting the human being in direct or indirect relation with something beyond his individuality that belongs to other states of existence.

In many cases the communication established is not even conscious although it is absolutely real.

When the Initiate Brother is going to work in order to open the doors of his inner Temple to himself, the rite re-focuses the condition in which he found himself straight after the initiation, which is the Silence. This will re-create the ideal conditions for a fruitful work.

We can say, then, that the Silence becomes the path used by the Initiate Brother to get in touch with the higher states; thanks to it he will acquire Knowledge.

The latter, which is the direct knowledge of the Transcendent, is in itself incommunicable and inexpressible; every expression used to transmit it is a formal and therefore human instrument and it is obviously inadequate to represent it.[13]

The Silence becomes also an attentive guardian of the acquisitions achieved by the Initiate. It becomes the case where the jewels of Knowledge are kept.

The Synthesis

We have already said that the spiritual power of Silence is great. Without it the Word is not possible and therefore truth, seriousness and life are not possible either.

For the Initiate Brother Silence is not a sterile gap but a fertile reflection; it is not an end in itself but it generates consequences. Therefore the Master will be able to make Silence inside himself for every step he wants to make; on the other hand, when he will be immersed in the profane world and he will picture himself as a Civil Man, he will necessarily need it to distill and make more understandable the transparent Temple inside him.

Through his soul's transparency he will bring in the profane world and the human dimension the precious material effects of the Light of Initiation; the latter will turn from the virtual into the real and he will have then accomplished this part of his duty and commitment as a Mason.

---

[13] Guénon writes: "human language is strictly connected to the practice of rational faculty for its own nature. As a consequence, all that is expressed or translated through this language naturally takes a form of 'reasoning', more or less explicitly." – And again: "...such a simply theoretical knowledge is obtained through the mental process, whilst effectual knowledge occurs 'through the spirit and the soul', viz. through the whole being".

THE CHAMBER OF REFLECTION

By: Giovanni Lombardo

The Chamber of Reflection is one of Freemasonry's most alluring, thought provoking and truly esoteric symbols. The Ancient and Accepted Scottish Rite (AASR) prescribes the profane, before being initiated, should enter a special room which is called Chamber of Reflection (CoR) where they will contemplate why they have chosen to embark on the Masonic path, their life, their past, and their future.

The word "reflection" as employed in the Chamber of Reflection has its etymological meaning from the Latin *reflectere,* to bend over, inwardly, so to explore one's own inner and discover the god that lies inside each of us. There he will examine himself, his motives and draw up his spiritual testament by answering the three great questions of human existence: "What are your duties toward:

A) the Supreme Being?
B) Yourself?
C) Humankind?"

The CoR echoes alchemy; and its furniture recalls many alchemical symbols. As there are many (especially in American Blue Lodges) who have not seen the CoR in use as part of an initiation we will being with a discussion of the Alchemical symbology employed therein, before moving on to a description of the CoR and its usages of those alchemical symbols

First of all, despite what many may have read or been taught, Alchemy is not magic; it is a symbolic science and an art, which is a philosophical approach. This approach is quite different from the common philosophy, and can be synopsized as: *Omnia ab uno et in unum omnia*, viz. "all is in one and one is in all".

Alchemy is a science dealing with material things aiming to a spiritual goal, for spirit and matter are but two opposite expressions or poles of the eternal. In truth, there is no difference between matter and spirit, as Cartesius taught, no separation between body and soul. Reality is the emanation of the One, whom we indirectly know through Nature. Even the word we use to describe everything, "universe", stems from Latin *universus,* "turned toward one".

Taking this concept to its next logical step we must therefore understand: All things in the universe are interrelated. Antoine Faivre called this the "doctrine of correspondences". This means that everything can, to a greater or lesser extent, influence, or be influenced by, every other thing. This is because Nature is a living entity, dynamic, multilevel, and multivalent and at all points interrelated.

This is particularly obvious in Spagyria, or Vegetal Alchemy. Spagyric products win the test of the monochromatic light of sodium, refracting such frequencies of light which assumes the form of a spiralling ray (think of a strand of the DNA molecule). This spiralling ray of light under sodium monochromatic light does not happen to chemically obtained medicines. Another feature of the spagyric products is their everlasting life, if they have been kept in safe custody, in a wooden box and far from light.

Alchemy is also a transmutative science. Transmutation is the change or conversion of both the agent-subject and the matter-object into something new and different. To transmute means that there is a modification of the subject in its very being, *i. e.* ontologically. Nonetheless, it is also a spiritual science, since the alchemist aims to create a living creature, thus repeating a cosmogony. In other words, he endeavours through alchemy to imitate the creative principle inherent in God. This is the biggest difference between alchemy and ordinary chemistry. The task of the alchemist is not to recombine atoms and molecules, but, rather, to purify matter. This goal cannot be reached but by the sheer power of the mind by one who has already purified himself.

Franz Hartmann wrote: "Alchemy, in its highest aspect, deals with the spiritual regeneration of man and teaches how a god may be made out of a human being or, to express it more correctly, how to establish the conditions necessary for the development of divine powers in man, so that a human being may became a god by the power of God in the same sense that a seed becomes a plant by the aid of the Four Elements and the action of the invisible Fifth Element (the Quintessence or Life Force)."

Aurum nostrum non est aurum vulgi, Our gold is not the common gold, said ancient alchemists, thus alluding to their own purification. They called those who merely sought after material power and riches "puffers". The gold of alchemy was simply hastened perfection, inner and outer, the divinization of matter and man. Purifying both man and matter implicates a process of death-rebirth. As Alchemy put matter in the *crucibulum*—an earthenware pot on burning fire, to separate the metals' various parts — *solve,* divide — and then to recombine them into a new substance — *coagula,* unite — so Freemasonry requires the neophyte be shut up in the CoR and purified of profanity's scum before being introduced in the Temple, purified and ready for light.

The profane is placed in the CoR, with various symbols of life and change. Upon the walls are written many phrases, designed to create serious and melancholy reflection, to engender in the profane thoughts of his place in nature, before God and man. Let us examine them closer.

* * *

In the CoR begins first symbolic journey of the Candidate, the journey into the earth, a traditional symbol employed in the initiatic tradition, symbolizing, as it does, the return to the beginning of life, to the womb. It is a narrow chamber, built according to the ratio 1:2, which is the same ratio as we find in the Temple of Solomon, and many temples from history. At first sight, the cavern symbolizes the womb and the process of gestation of the profane that is going to abandon his old being to be reborn to a new life, in the same way as the chrysalis has to die, so that the butterfly can exist. To reinforce the concept of the return to the beginning, to the womb, and to demonstrate the candidate is in darkness prior to being brought to a new light in the lodge, the floor, walls and ceiling of the CoR are painted an opaque black.

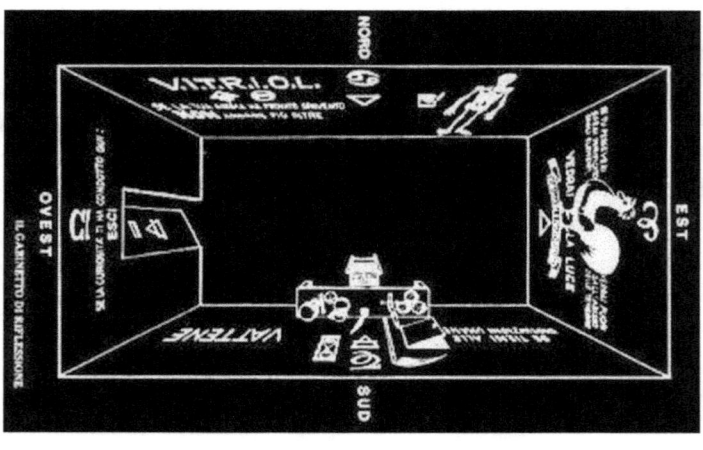

* * *

On the North wall (from which begins the symbolic first journey) — are painted the zodiacal sign of the Cancer the Crab (which represents Solstice in summer, and is blue in colour), a human Skeleton, the acrostic V.I.T.R.I.O.L., the alchemical symbols of Sulphur and Salt, and an Oil-lamp. Electrical light should never be used. The hermetic philosophers only used an oil-lamp with an asbestos wick. It is easy to use and gives a uniform heat. This is the fire they have been hiding so much and nobody openly mentioned. On the plane of Spiritual Alchemy, the Fire is made up by the Prayer: *Ora et Labora,* pray and work. The word "laboratory" echoes the Benedictine motto.

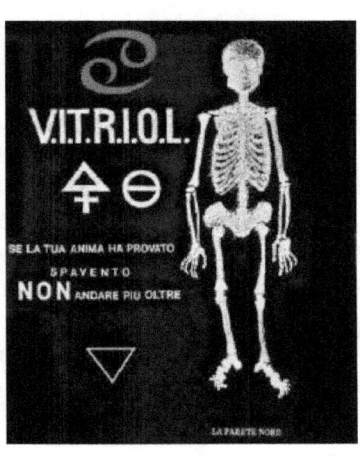

V.I.T.R.I.O.L. means *Visita Interiora Terræ Rectificandoque Invenies Occultum Lapidem* Visit the interior of the earth, and, rectifying, purifying it, you will find the hidden stone. Some other read *Visita Interiora Tua…*, visit your own interior or soul, but the meaning is the same. At this stage, in fact, the Recipient identifies himself with matter, thus earth; the (Masonic) spirituality is still far from him. He must go down in the deepest of his soul, to know himself firstly: Know Thyself. The skeleton symbolizes the bare man, alone with himself, without any psychological defences. To know oneself, that is, to be aware of one's own true essence, is however not enough: the Candidate, or "Man of Wish", has to correct his flaws. Later he must become "Man of Will", and in doing so, he will find the treasure which has been hidden inside himself, namely, the Inner Master — or God — which lies within each man. The task is not simple: man needs courage. This is the reason for the warning we find on the wall. Man needs courage and strength. This does not mean have no fear — only fools have no fear for fear is a great teacher when properly harnessed — but rather, to have enough strength to go beyond it. Salt and Sulphur are symbols of matter and spirit respectively. Since the Initiate's task consists in balancing them through Mercury, it is expedient he does so from the beginning, when he is in the

Chamber of Reflection. There we find only symbolic references to Mercury, which otherwise would be absent. Mercury represents the intelligence, the communication. The god Mercury has a pair of wings onto his feet; he is the gods' messenger. In Alchemy, it is associated to Air and Water. Painted on the wall is the following sentence:

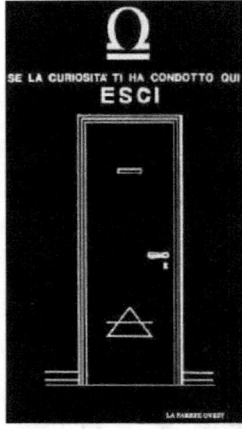

IF YOUR SOUL IS FRIGHTENED: DO NOT CONTINUE

Below this is the hermetic symbol of Water, for every gestation needs water. Water also symbolizes man's emotional part. The Candidate is left in total solitude, for at this point, he cannot profit by any outside help, he must work on his inner self by himself and suffer purification by separation: *Pathémata Mathémata*, suffering is teaching, said the ancient Greeks.

* * *

The candidate enters via the West, and on this wall is painted the zodiacal sign of Libra the scale of balance (Equinox in autumn, yellow colour) and the following sentence:

IF CURIOSITY BROUGHT YOU HERE: LEAVE!

Below this is the hermetic symbol of Air.

This element means intelligence; it refers itself to mind and any intellectual activity, therefore knowledge. It may appear strange, therefore, the negative reference to curiosity, this being the first and probably also the best stick to gain knowledge. Curiosity, here, is not the true wish of knowledge. Curiosity is meant to boost one's ego. The knowledge which Freemasons should long for, is instead the preliminary step to act, to build both the inner Temple, firstly, and then that of humankind. "A man who leaves home to mend himself and others is a philosopher; but he who goes from country to country, guided by the blind impulse of curiosity, is a vagabond", wrote Oliver Goldsmith. The inner Temple must be balanced with the outer one. Balance references Libra and thence to the Equinox. Equinox stems from Latin: *æqua nox,* that is, the night is equal to the day; they last the same time, being absolutely balanced.

* * *

The South wall is painted with the zodiacal sign of Capricorn, the Ram (Solstice in winter, green color), a Scythe, which refers to Saturn, the Lord of Time, and the Hourglass. There is also a little Window with a Mirror (the Mirror can also be covered by a tent or curtain). Also on the wall is the hermetic symbol for Earth. Painted on the wall is the following sentence:

> IF YOU CARE ABOUT HUMAN DISTINCTIONS: GO OUT!

On the table are set an Inkwell made of crystal containing China black ink with a (Goose) Quill Pen, a Candle; 3 little Bowls (made of wood or clay) containing Salt, Sulphur and Sand; a piece of stale Bread; a Pitcher of water; a human Skull and crossbones. The table is rectangular and 72 cm high and painted in opaque black, it is set against the wall; the candleholder is 22 cm. high. Symbols that have been painted here are mainly those of time. The hourglass reminds us that human life is ephemeral, subject to death, which is symbolized by the scythe. This latter, however, is also symbols of Universal Justice, for "as we sow, so shall we reap". The mirror alludes to our inner selves, our spirits and to self examination. It is often covered by a tent, curtains, or a window, so as to implicitly invite the Candidate to open it and to see his image reflected in it. This alludes to a deeply esoteric teaching: Man's worst enemy is often himself, and also that we should seek within.

When Buddha fought against the cobra, the latter suddenly took on the semblance of the former. This taught us that while we often blame our brother over the mote in his eye, unaware of the beam which sticks out our own. It is from this perspective man must read the warning on this wall. Human distinctions are an obstacle to creating and keeping true brotherhood. Unfortunately, they exist even in Freemasonry. The rejection of candidates for either on religious or racial grounds is still a plague, an unbearable shame for an institution which strives to be "universal". Within our ranks are men who long for sashes and collars, thinking that if they can wear them they will be more important, more glamorous than those who cannot. This is a childish, unworthy, small and unmasonic goal, one which displays immaturity, inner poverty and little else. The China black ink and the goose quill recall the vegetal reign and the animal one, respectively, again, alchemical balance, and is present for the candidate to use in answering the questions. Sand is present to highlight the sterile room, as if it would protect the Candidate from any external influence. Salt and Sulphur are symbols of matter and spirit respectively and their physical presence echoes and amplifies the symbols on the wall. Bread and water are the simplest food for everybody. There is a clear reference to simplicity, as we can also see in the Fool, one of the Tarots' Major Arcanes.

The Fool, like the Candidate, is a man undertaking a journey; his packsaddle is small because he has taken the few essential things. At his heels, an impulse — the dog biting at his leg — pushes him onwards. The staff in his hand is seen blossoming, meaning that he is about to gain new riches, not material riches, but spiritual for the journey of the Fool is the spiritual journey of change and growth. Bread is a symbol of transmutation (death) gained through hard work: *Verily, verily, I say unto you, except a corn of wheat fall into the ground and die, it abideth alone: but if it die, it bringeth forth much fruit...* (John: XII, 24). Bread also symbolizes the "Great Work" to be done by the Candidate before being initiated and, above all, afterwards, to subdue his passions — symbolized by Water — and to sublimate them to higher plans of the Being. The Human Skull symbolizes the highest part of the human body: every and all alchemic operation brings its effects into it. Next to the skull are crossed thigh bones, which in Egyptian mythology, were the siege of *Ka*.

Ka was considered to be the essential ingredient or dimension that differentiated a living person from a dead one. Difficult to directly translate, it is possibly one of the most concise interpretations is "life force" or "sustenance". The *Ka* is represented in hieroglyphs by a pair of arms pointing upwards. In modern, scientific terms, *Ka* might be compared to DNA. Alchemy aimed to transmute it through appropriate operations and to sublimate the bodily essence in harmony with mental faculties. Furthermore, the crossed bones might be interpret as a reference to coitus, which is to be meant as *conjunctio oppositorum,* uniting what is opposite, to go beyond duality and to restore unity. The symbols contained on the table should be interpreted in light of the table itself. The table is 72 cm tall and the candleholder 22 cm., numbers which have deeper meaning in themselves. Hebrew Cabalists describe the seventy-two names of God. By reading the Bible, they came across a unique phenomenon in the whole Torah: three consecutive verses, each of them having seventy-two letters. They are Exodus: 14, 19-21 and describe the culminant phase of parting the Red Sea. Seventy-two is the numerical value of the Hebrew word: *Chesed*, Love, and in fact the help of God on the occasion of the parting of the Red Sea and the salvation of the Hebrews must be considered as an act of Love. By combining such letters, they got seventy-two names which match so many faculties of the Almighty. Twenty-two are the letters of the Hebrew alphabet. Like Egyptians, Jews knew the power of the word. *Ma-kehru*, the right voice, was how the Egyptian priest was known. This was the priest who was able to modulate his voice in such a way as to emit vibrations which would excite a specific "faculty" of the One, thus getting His aid in any specific circumstance of his earthly life. What is important is not what is said, but, rather, how it is said. By the way, this still happens today by reciting the Psalms in Latin, since Saint Jerome paid great attention to preserve this faculty of speech when he wrote the *Vulgata*. In conclusion, the Candidate gets the following teaching from a careful examination and contemplation of the symbols on this wall: man can rely on God's love and get His help on condition that he is able to speak to Him: The *quaerite et invenietis* [seek, and ye shall find] of the Gospel is therefore no vain saying.

* * *

The East wall is emblazoned with the zodiacal sign of the Aries, the Ram (Equinox in spring, red color), a Rooster crowing, and the following: (left side of the Observer) IF YOU PERSIST IN, YOU SHALL BE PURIFIED FROM THE ELEMENTS
(right side of the Observer) YOU SHALL COME OUT FROM THE ABYSS OF THE DARKNESS
(in the middle) YOU SHALL SEE THE LIGHT
Under the Rooster, in a flag, are the words: VIGILANCE AND PERSEVERANCE

Below all the other symbols are the hermetic symbol for Fire. Let's consider the two sentences, starting from the one on the left side. Alchemists thought the four natural Elements from which all other proceeded were Water (Hydrogen) – Air (Azoth) – Fire (Oxygen) – Earth (Carbon) corresponded to the four qualities: Humid – Hot – Dry – Cold, and to the four Temperaments: Sanguine – Bilious – Nervous – Lymphatic. Every man is a mixture of four elements, such a mixture being his feature or nature. However, some elements are stronger in one man than the others. For instance, Air being related to the "mental". It is therefore possible he who has it in an overriding quantity can go astray, led by fanciful thoughts. What the candidate needs to learn is if he perseveres in walking the inner path, he will learn how to balance the elements, to get rid of the worst aspects of each of them — to smooth his Rough Ashlar — thus harmonizing his personality, and his life. One again, balance between the material and the spiritual. The second sentence clearly alludes to the psychological "process of individuation". Abyss, from Greek *abyssos,* literally "bottomless", in psychology means the "collective unconscious", the values of a group which man has unconsciously absorbed during his early life. Through the process of individuation he will find his own values, that make him an individual, that is, a unique entity, which can no more be divided — Latin: *indivisus* — an integrated personality, master of his life and of his destiny. It is a process of self realization during which one integrates those contents of the psyche that have the ability to become conscious. It is a search for totality and a balance between them that creates the integrated personality, one not tending one way or the other. If the Candidate learns the lessons taught in the CoR, he shall see the Light, that is, God. He shall "know" Him, becoming one within the One. The song of the Rooster announces the rebirth of the sun, or the return of the great light also symbolically announces the Candidate's "resurrection" or rebirth from the womb. The Rooster's crowing recommends vigilance and perseverance, symbolized by the long vigil through the night for the rebirth of the sun which the Rooster holds daily. Vigilance means to watch oneself with patience, to avoid arrogance for good results — if any — so gained; perseverance is the continuation of the journey on the inner path: research and learning are endless, indeed.

The Tyler shall watch the Candidate through the peephole to ascertain when he has completed his will and answers to the questions. When this is done, the Marshal shall bring his testament to the Worshipful Master, who will read it for the final approval by the Brethren. Once this is received, the Candidate shall be duly prepared (bare left foot, right knee, chest) a cable-tow on his neck and introduced in the Temple: the ceremony of initiation then begins.

ORIENTATIONS AND PERAMBULATIONS

By: Giovanni Lombardo

To orientate, or to orient, means to face or turn to the east, to the rising sun, thus receiving light and heat, that were, especially in ancient times, the primary source of energy. So, men used to orient themselves to face the east, the sun, in order to receive energy and then balance it inwardly.

According to the far eastern tradition, the universe was made essentially by *Yin* and *Yang,* the two principles of opposing energies and states balancing each other. *Yin* is the feminine principle, while *Yang* is the masculine one. They act as two poles, negative and positive, which must be considered rather more complementary than opposite.[1]

They are the two poles of the Manifestation, earth and heaven, night and day, male and female and so on. They can be also considered as the main sources of any stream of energy – like electricity, for instance. *Yin* and *Yang* are in perennial dialectics and life is the relevant outcome, as we can see every day.

Duality is therefore a feature of the manifestation, while unity is that of the Immutable Being. The initiate strives to restore unity, symbolically starting from his earthly life. Hence the importance of catching the outer energy, balancing it with the inner one. To orient oneself properly is just one of the means through which this goal can be achieved.

On this subject, Bro. René Guénon writes:

"In the primordial age man was perfectly balanced in himself in terms of yin *and* yang. *What is more, he was* yin *or passive in relation to the Principle alone, and* yang *or active in relation to the Cosmos, or the totality of manifested things. Hence he naturally turned to the North, which is* yin, *as the complementary to him.*

---

[1] Cf. *Chain of Union*, in Lodgeroom International Magazine, July 2006

By way of contrast, because of the spiritual degeneration occurring in the descending course of the cycle, the man of later ages became yin *in relation to the Cosmos. He must therefore turn to the South, which is* yang, *to receive from it the influences of the principle complementary to the one which has become predominant inside him, and to restore as much as possible the equilibrium between* yin *and* yang.

The first of these two orientations can be called 'polar', in contrast to the second, which is 'solar'. In the first, man faces towards the Pole Star, North, or 'pinnacle of heaven', with the east to his right and the west to his left. In the second case he faces towards the Sun at the meridian, with the East to his left and the West to his right. Here we have the explanation for an apparent anomaly in the Far-Eastern tradition which can be very disconcerting for those who are not aware of its cause"[2]

Of course, when we speak of left and right, we must consider these terms vary, depending on the prospective we are considering. Usually, left and right are those of the observer. So, for example, in the Kabalistic diagram showing the 'sephirotic tree', the right pillar and the left pillar are respectively to one's right and to one's left looking at the diagram.

In the western tradition, the right side is favorable. In old Greek *déxios*, from which the Latin *dexter*, meaning 'skilled' or able to act well. The English 'right' evokes the Plumb of the Great Architect and Justice. To the contrary *lævus*, left, is joint to the Greek *làios*, which means "bent toward earth," and therefore the evocation of 'cripple' or 'wounded'.

Before we go on to the next concept, we should look at the scalene triangle, which will be important. A scalene triangle is a triangle with a different length on each side. The word scalene comes from the Greek *skalénos,* which

---

[2] René Guénon, *The Great Triad*, Quinta Essentia, Cambridge 1991 p. 51

means unequal and tortuous, and so evokes the concept of deviousness.

In China, in ancient times left was considered the preeminent side: "In matters that are favorable (or of good omen) the left is placed uppermost, but in affairs that are ill-omened, the right".[3] There was a change thereafter, probably in correspondence of a change of dynasty. In any case, whichever orientation is adopted – polar or solar, so to have East respectively to the right side or to the left one – East is invariably the most important side, it being considered the source of light.

The foregoing explains the reason why in Masonic symbolism the Lodge is not supposed to have any windows or light in the North (this being the side that never directly receives solar light), a place that is masonically in darkness. There is, however, light in the East, South and West, which correspond to the three 'stations' of the Sun, and of the three principle officers of the lodge, the Worshipful Master, the Senior and Junior Wardens.

Actually, the Worshipful Master seats at East, but in the Operatives' tradition the Solomon's throne was put at West, so to face the 'rising sun'. I could not find any explanation for this inversion. Maybe the Worshipful Master, so doing, intended to receive the light and the energy of the sun, as a container, to later avail himself of these gifts during the construction of the edifice.

* * *

Another issue directly related to orientation is the direction of ritual perambulation. The direction determines whether the orientation is 'polar' or 'solar' (using these words in the sense in which we used them above). A diagram will help us to understand this matter better.

---

[3] *Tao Te Ching,* chapter 31

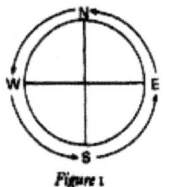
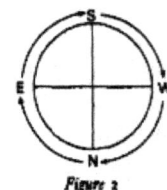

Figure 1   Figure 2

Figure 1 shows the direction in which the stars appear to orbit the pole when man faces the North; figure 2 shows the direction of the apparent movement of the sun for an observer facing South. In the first case, the perambulation is performed keeping the centre to one's left, thus counter clockwise, called *widdershin* in Middle Low German, a word which literally means "to go against". In figure 2, the perambulation is performed keeping the centre of the lodge on one's right (called *pradakshina* in Sanskrit and *deosil* in Gaelic), and is a clockwise movement.

This second modality is the one adopted chiefly in the Hindu and Tibetan traditions, while the former is found mainly in the near eastern and western tradition. Bro. Guénon noted *"it is perhaps not without interest to point out that the direction of these circumambulations proceeding respectively from left to right and from right to left also corresponds to the direction of the script in the sacred languages of these same traditional forms. In the present form of Masonry, the direction of the 'circumambulations' is 'solar'; but it seems on the contrary to have been 'polar' in the ancient 'operative' ritual"*.[4]

Bound up with this difference of the ritual circumambulation is the question of whether the walker should *start* out with the right or left foot. According to Bro. Guénon, it is *"obvious that the foot which has to be put forward first will be the one opposite to the side facing in towards the centre of the circumambulation";* that is, starting off on the right foot in the case of figure 1 traveling counter-clockwise, and with the left in the case of figure 2, traveling clockwise. This tradition seems to be generally the case, even when it is not strictly speaking a question of circumambulation as such. It

---

[4] René Guénon, *The Solstitial Doors*, in *Symbols of Sacred Science*, footnote 5, Sophia Perennis, Hillsadale NY, 1991

is more likely simply an indication of the predominance of either the 'polar' or the 'solar' perspective. In other words, whether the ritual is to start with the left and travels counter-clockwise or with the left and travel clockwise, the unwritten tradition of the culture. This predominance may be associated with a particular traditional form, or it can sometimes even vary at different periods in the span of existence of one and the same tradition."[5] One can see many examples of this in how one is supposed to approach the altar, starting with the left foot in Western and near eastern tradition, and with the right in far eastern traditions. It can also be seen in military rank and file marching, where in the west, soldiers always start off with the left foot, a deeply ingrained and really unnoticed behavior.

* * *

The last – and complementary question – is whether Brethren have to square the Temple when they walk inside it. In my opinion they should, for the following reasons.

The Temple's shape is a rectangle, built in 1:2 ratio. If we trace the diagonal, we obtain two right triangles. From the Pythagorean Theorem, we know that in any right triangle, the square of the length of the hypotenuse (the side of a right triangle opposite the right angle) is equal to the sum of the squares of lengths of the two legs.

Conversely, the metric value of the hypotenuse shall be

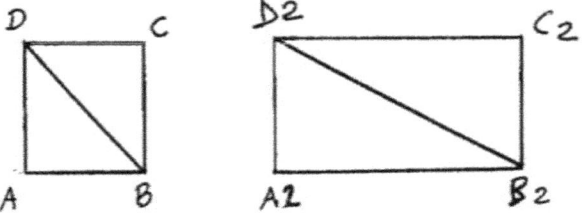

equal to its square root. In the first figure, assuming 1 as length of each side, it shall be square root 2, so 1,41; in the

---

[5] René Guénon, *The Great Triad*, cit. p. 56

second figure it shall be square root 5 ($1^2+2^2=1+4=5$), which is equal to 2,2360.

This number corresponds to the proportion with which the various parts of the human body develop in man's phase of growth. By squaring the Temple we are therefore reminded of this reality, thus strengthening the idea of progressive growth at intellectual, moral and spiritual level.

Orientation, perambulation and squaring are therefore just three phases of the same process. In order to catch energy, to balance it inwardly in respect of the 'centre' and eventually to use it for the harmonic construction of our Temple, the beauty of which will recall us the true splendor of Truth.

SQUARE AND COMPASSES

By: Giovanni Lombardo

In esoteric Gnosis, symbols have many meanings. They are the product of the human being who, consciously or unconsciously, expresses spirituality in the metaphysical or physical reality.

Gnòsis (from the Greek word for knowledge) is used in English to specify the spiritual knowledge of a saint or enlightened human being. It is described as the direct experiential knowledge of the supernatural or divine. This is not enlightenment understood in its general sense of insight or learning (which in Greek is *diafotisthoùn*) but enlightenment that validated the existence of the supernatural.

The Oxford English Dictionary defines it as, 'A knowledge of spiritual mysteries'. From the word *gnosis* is derived Gnostic and Gnosticism the latter a modern construct referring to one of various near eastern schools which claimed to have supernatural knowledge flourishing during the early Christian era. The term being *Koine* Greek has, nonetheless, a much broader application than being exclusive to any sectarian group. The term is used by Byzantine and Hellenic cultures as a word to mean a special knowledge or insight of the supernatural. In some sense mature understanding or knowledge. It is the knowledge that comes from experience rather than from rational or reasoned thinking as in intuitive knowledge.[1]

Symbols are tied to fundamental archetypes, common to various époques, so man can infer they belong to a hereditary Tradition. They are not, however, revealed truths or they have any magical power.

Symbols are objects, characters, or other concrete representations of ideas, concepts, or other abstractions. In more psychological and philosophical terms, every percep-

---

[1] From Wikipedia, the free encyclopedia
http://en.wikipedia.org/wiki/Gnosis

tion is symbolic, and humans often react to symbolism on a subconscious level.

In the esoteric context – free from any religious doctrine – symbols are instruments to arouse thoughts and feelings, which the initiates shall develop afterwards, thinking over them. The square and the compasses are the emblem *par excellence* of Freemasonry, be it either Ancient – operative – or Modern, speculative and with the VSL they form the three great lights of Freemasonry.

The square evokes other symbols, such as the Cross, in particular the Tau: T, which can be also turned upside down: ⊥. Four squares form the Latin cross: +

Sometimes the square arms are of different length; usually they reflect the ratio 1:2, or 3:4, thus evoking the rectangle. Let us think of the Pythagorean rectangle, the sides of which are 3, 4, and 5 units, or of the Greek Delta: △, this being the form of the Greek temples' pediment.

The square symbolizes the matter: let us think of the four cardinal points, the four rivers of the earthly paradise, the four figures lying at the Lamb's feet, in *Revelation*, and so on. It is also symbol of solidity: the cube, or better of inner solidity, thus of morality. A man cannot work well outside of himself if he has not previously put order within. By the square, a man smoothes his own rough ashlar, removing those rough places which do not let him to live in harmony within himself and with his neighbors.

The square is matter, immovable, thus feminine, while the compasses are movable, thus masculine. The square belongs to mankind, it represents the womb from which we all spring, while the G.A.O.T.U. owns the compasses, which are the spirit.

The two arms of the square evoke duality which is the simplest aspect of the reign of the mortal, physical manifestation of our lives. By the square, we build "shelter", that which is 'enclosed' like our lives, from beginning to end.

If we examine the compasses, we can immediately see it's divine feature: All geometrical construction starts from the center, a dimensionless point. This dimensionless point is the symbol of the One which is outside space and time. It is (in) the eternity.

The circle is the point's projection; it is the One that creates the multiplicity. In the *Comedy* Dante stated it quite clearly:

> *Then it began "The One who turned His compass*
> *to mark the world's confines, and in them set*
> *so many things concealed and things revealed*
>
> *could not imprint His Power into all*
> *the universe without His Word remaining*
> *in infinite excess of such a vessel."*[2]

By joining the square to the circle we connect heaven and earth, the spiritual with the material, thus creating a new symbol, that of the cosmic sacred wedding from which union Masonic initiates are born:

> *I am parched with thirst, and perishing,*
> *But drink of me, the ever-flowing spring on the right,*
> *(where) there is a fair cypress.*
> *Who are you? Where are you from?*
> *I am a child of Earth and of starry Heaven, but my*
> *race is of Heaven (alone).*
> (Orphic Lamella from Thessaly)

The same idea is displayed in Far-Eastern traditions, for instance, in the *Bushido,* the *samurais'* code of honor.

When the compasses are spread at ninety degrees, the section so formed by the radii is the fourth part of the circle and the square is back once again. It is, however, a renewed square, imbued of spiritual afflatus: human morality is meaningless, or at least poor if spirituality does not wrap it.

The spread of compasses legs then symbolizes the initiate's broad-mindedness, which is not only confined to mental activity but is also extended to spiritual search. We

---

[2] Dante Alighieri, *Comedy*, Paradiso, Translated by Mandelbaum, Canto 19:40-45

can spread the compasses legs progressively, but not indefinitely. This means that knowledge is progressive, but the initiate is to be aware of his own limits. Knowledge always implies humility.

In the Craft degrees, the compasses are spread at 45°, and a Past Master is represented by the compasses, at 60° and an ARC rather than a square, symbolizing that the master has risen above the material plain. In some of the higher degrees of the A.A.S.R. the compasses are spread to 60° or 90°. In no case may the compasses be spread more than 179°, since they would thereafter become a straight line, which recalls the Plumb, symbol of divine justice.

In Middle-Ages and in Renaissance architects and artists used proportional compasses, by which they obtained any and all architectural drawings. It is for this very reason that we can find the compasses in some rites, beyond the Craft, to exalt the human creative intelligence which can range anywhere, free from ignorance, superstition and prejudices.[3]

The square and the compasses are over the VSL, thus meaning that the pure metaphysical knowledge is superior in respect of any positive religion.

Eventually, the square and the compasses, united, give us a most distinctive idea of the unity of the material and the spiritual, and by contemplating them we can thus apply those tools to our situations, thus realizing our goal of ascending beyond the material and improving our spirits, which is what makes us better men.

---

[3] *E. g.* in the Tracing-Board of Rito Simbolico Italiano

THE TESSELLATED PAVEMENT

By: Roberto Fivizzani

*I swear by the night when it draws a veil,
And the day when it shines in brightness,
And the creating of the male and the female...*

Koran 92:1-3

The tessellated pavement, or mosaic pavement, is a rectangle, the longer side oriented along the East-West axis. In some lodges it is located in the centre of the Temple, and in others it extends the whole length of the temple, starting from the two pillars Boaz and Jachin, which symbolize essence and substance, respectively, hence the pair of opposites that rule the whole of manifestation.

I think there is deeper symbolic meaning in the central placement. The pavement of the lodge then has two parts. The central part, which is bordered by white and black tiles, represents the possibilities of manifestation which one encounters in life, and the remainder, conversely, represents the non-manifested possibilities, so that the pavement as a whole symbolizes the universal possibility, be it manifest or non-manifest. It follows that the lodge opens its business at a metaphysical level.

Essence and substance are the active and passive principles, symbolized by the white and black tiles respectively, male and female. Essence (white) contains the possibilities which shall develop, availing themselves of substance, that is, form (black).[1]

Let us think about an idea and the way to put it in words: the idea still exists, even without the words, but it cannot do without them if it is to be expressed; conversely,

---

[1] The term "substance" is to be interpreted in its etymological meaning, from Latin *sub-stare*, "to stay under", so to support, to hold up [Ed.]

some written words without an idea would be just meaningless signs. In conclusion, essence is a 'principle' in relation to substance, which is its material support.

Among the various dualities, let me recall "I" and "you", the subject and the object; the inner, the white tile, and the external, the black tile, which apparently oppose and limit each other reciprocally, since everybody considers himself as subject and others as object, that is, different from him.

The Tao begat one, one begat two, two begat three and three begat the ten thousand things; the ten thousand things carry Yin and embrace Yang and through their blending of forces they achieve harmony.

The Tao referred to here is the passive Tao, the Void (*wu*), which gives rise to the one, the active Tao, the Supreme Reality, which produces the manifestation. Its aspects all seem to be in conflict with each other, so they need the presence of a balancing principle in order to give birth to harmony.

The Sacred Law, being the lawful expression of the Supreme Reality, guarantees equilibrium and harmony; for this reason the altar – and the VSL which is laid over it – is over the pavement.

Other opposites are freedom and necessity, will and destiny, ignorance and knowledge. The white tile symbolizes freedom, will and knowledge, which are within the subject; need, destiny and ignorance are represented by the black tile and are beside the object, which cannot be known for it is beyond free will. It therefore appears as destiny.

The tessellated pavement reminds us of the game of chess: each player can freely move his pieces, but each move entails consequences which limit his ability to choose further. The same happens in ordinary life, where actions engender consequences which are sometimes irreversible, so that the final event will seem to be destiny's decision.

Another symbolic parallel worthy of note: in chess, the axial movement of the rook, the diagonal movement of the bishop, and the leaping movement of the knight, correspond respectively to the Entered Apprentice, Fellow of the

Craft, and Master Mason. The king, who can go anywhere, is like those Past Masters, living symbols of undivided essence who therefore can sit wherever they wish. Rectilinear movement, from one square to another, recalls the progression of those beings who are not yet free and therefore walk across the stream of forms, passing through a plurality of deaths (black) and rebirths (white), while diagonal movement, and even more movement by leaps, marks a discontinuity which lets man go beyond the manifold manifestation and reach the Immutable Centre "from which a Master Mason cannot err".

In the ritual of the Entered Apprentice's initiation, we find a hint of the Centre: the points of the compasses are laid on the candidate's heart. The heart symbolises the Centre, being the seat of intellectual intuition.[2] The candidate, by means of the initiation, becomes a new centre, and therefore will open the compasses progressively, so as to incorporate the 'object' which appeared to be separate from himself.

In *Man and his becoming according to Vedanta*, René Guénon writes that any and all aspects of the Manifestation are hierarchically ordered, from the Universal, which embraces also "subtle" states, thus invisible, to the Individual, which can be even the humblest earthly element.

At the highest level, the single man identifies himself with the single idea, the archetype which displays the principle in its simplest form.

Then, going backwards, man finds the Individual, which can be either collective or singular. A lodge, for instance, is a collective individuality, formed by the Brothers who are enrolled within it. They are, indeed, still distinct from each other, but no longer separated, because they are in harmony with the Centre.

The General and the Particular sum up every individuality, thus implementing the Lesser Mysteries. Beyond this

---

[2] Using the term "intellectual" in Guénon's sense of supra-rational direct apprehension, as contrasted with empirical knowledge. [ED]

step there is eventually the Universal, the non-manifested possibility.

Replying to objections drawn from the plurality of beings, René Guénon wrote: "The being that has realized the integrality of a state has itself become the centre of that state, and, this being the case, one may say that it fills this state entirely with its own irradiation; it assimilates to itself all that is contained therein, making of it so many secondary modalities of itself, as it were, comparable somewhat to the modalities that are realized in the dream state... The whole of that state is constituted only by the irradiation of its centre, and any being effectively positioned at this centre by this very fact becomes master of the state in its integrality; thus the 'principial'[3] indifferentiation of the non-manifested is reflected in the manifested, it being clearly understood that the reflection retains the relativity inherent in all conditioned existence, since it is in the manifested realm".[4]

The starry heaven, like the chequered pavement, symbolizes the multiplicity. The heaven contains two distinct symbolic elements, that is, the stars, which correspond to the supra-formal elements, and, in the background, the simple blue heaven, without any stars, symbolizing the metaphysical essence, the goal of any ascension. The pavement thus represents the earth, the starting point, while the heaven represents the final goal.

The realization gained by the initiation would not be complete if it did not entail the "descending" phase, from heaven to earth, from the One to multiplicity.

---

[3] *Principial*: of the *Principe*, the primary Source and Origin of everything. An example of Guénon's idiosyncratic vocabulary. [ED]
[4] R. Guénon, *The multiple states of the being*, Sophia Perennis, Hillsdale, NY, pp. 75-76

Esoteric Masonic Thought

However, the man who comes back to earth no longer partakes of such multiplicity, for he has transcended any apparent oppositions. He is a true universal man, Hiram resurrected, whose head is in the light and whose feet firmly press on the tessellated pavement: the picture of the Mason whose body is made up of the lodge's tools displays this idea better than any words.

THE THREE PILLARS

By: Jean-Michel David

Many of our brethren on the continent of Europe may be puzzled even by the title: *three* columns or pillars? Certainly *two*, as pillars, is pretty much universally understood in Freemasonry, but there is something that is more peculiar - but not exclusive - to Freemasonic forms as developed especially in the Anglophonic world.

For those of us in that world, the inverse may very well be the case, with a sense of perplexity that a fellow Freemason seems befuzzled at the mention of the three pillars.

So firstly, let's make a clear distinction between the *two* pillars and the three: they are not related in the minds of many, and in various descriptions found in both ritual and documents. Having said this, there are of course many ways they can be found to be closely tied by both historical development and, perhaps more importantly for exegesis, by the active thinking imagination. I shall present one such perspective in this paper.

For the sake of those brethren who are not familiar with the three pillars, they are found *within* the Temple or Lodge room (I shall henceforth use the latter term by personal preference). In contradistinction, the *two* pillars are those that the Torah (the Pentateuch) tells us are placed at the porch way or entrance to King Solomon's Temple: they remain outside.

The three pillars, inside the Lodge room, also formerly provided the minimal amount of lighting required, upon which each bears a candle (or its modern equivalent: an electric bulb in too many parts of the world, inevitably losing the obvious sense that fire, or *passion*, gives rise to light). They thus provide the 'lesser lights'[1] to the room - the *greater* lights being symbolically provided by the VSL (or

---

[1] These were earlier called 'greater lights' but, in working compromise between the 'Antients' and the 'Moderns', were re-named.

sacred writing), the Square, and the Compasses. Here we already see that the *symbolic* and *internal* light is deemed of greater value than the external physical light, despite the fact that such physical light is also to be taken with its full symbolic sense of a triune of light over darkness.

So perhaps questions can be asked as to why one form of Freemasonry has these three, the another form does not. The answer appears to lie in historical developments of the various Lodge room arrangement and layout.[2] Below are typical general floor plans. I say 'typical' even though it should be pointed out that variations occurs on the basic same theme. In fact, chances are that the reader's own Lodge will differ somewhat from either of these. A third relatively common floor plan are for either the two or three pillars to be placed adjacent the tessellated pavement (when this does not occupy the *whole* floor space). Forget the green arrows in the floor plan diagrammes that follow for now - I'll refer to these in short enough time.

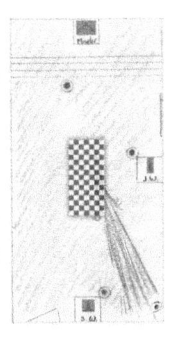

Diagramme A is more or less typical of many '*Continental*' European Lodge rooms, and B more or less typical of Anglo-Saxon ones. But remember, variations and cross-usage occurs.

I'll be referring to these in the discussion that follows. In each case, it should be noted that brethren are (with some exceptions) seated in the north and south sides.

Naming the pillars

On Floor Plan A, it should be obvious to any brother who has been passed that the two pillars refer to Boaz and Jachin (this latter transliterated from the Hebrew in various ways), and have further allusion to the pillars of fire and cloud that guided the Jews fleeing from their Egyptian

---

[2] *Cf.* B. Jones 1956, p. 355 *f*

bondage. Much more can be said of these, and reflection on 1 Kings 7 is encouraged.

On Floor Plan B, the three pillars, presented with lit candle atop each, refer to three orders of architecture: the Doric, Ionic, and Corinthian (with the Tuscan and what is called the 'composite' therefore omitted). Which column or pillar is placed adjacent the Master and the Wardens varies, though it has become commonplace to have the Ionic with the Master representing *Wisdom* (and hence easily associated with King Solomon); the Doric with the Senior Warden representing *Strength* (or *Fortitude*); and the Corinthian with the Junior Warden representing *Beauty*.

A symbolic distinction that can be gleaned between the two and three pillars, despite their otherwise possible reconciliation, is from observing the frontispiece from the *Scottish Constitution* of 1848.

Here we can not only see the three columns (as they are more generally referred to than 'pillars') in the foreground and similarly presented to the Harris standardised first degree tracing board (to which we shall return in a minute), as well as the two pillars (on the left of the image, deeper in perspective) referring to Boaz and Jachin.

It should be noted that the image has the Corinthian on the right-hand side, the Doric in the centre (and further set from the viewer's perspective), and the Ionic to the left. This is also, in fact, an example of the variation that I mentioned a couple of paragraphs above, for hereon the Master is presented with the Doric.

Compare this to the 1st degree tracing board that has become the standard (though definitely not the sole version) used in Lodges

Esoteric Masonic Thought

set according to Floorplan B - the basic design painted by John Harris *circa* 1845. Comparing here not only the three pillars in their respective positions, but also the location of Sun, Moon (with and without stars, and All-Seeing Eye or, in this case, the heptagramme (which is sometimes instead a pentalpha, ie, a pentagramme).

With both these images, what is also clear is that the working tools associated with the Master and the two Wardens are clearly placed at their respective base. The perspective is therefore presented without confusion: the viewer's position is from the deep South-West, in the place I have marked Floorplan B with an eye, and the arrow the direction of view.

If nothing else, the tracing board presents to the imaginative faculty a means to enter in meditative light the Lodge room, here presented too with altar and stairway or ladder towards the spiritual realms.

The overall pattern, however, is not closely connected to an 18th C. tracing board depicting more closely our Floorplan A. Observe, however, that the *three* virtues of Wisdom, Strength and Beauty are also preserved, and those with clearly Jachin and Boaz. In this case, the *Master* is allocated Beauty:

I have taken a little space to present these variations on both floor design, pillar variations, and the position of what can only be called three Masonic Virtues (on which a little more to come) in great part to show that any discussions at times presupposes a single viewpoint, rather than the variety that actually finds expression within the Craft. If Freemasonry encourages the meeting of people with vastly different religious and political views, then we should also give due consideration to the variety that presents itself within Freemasonry Universal.

Virtues

There appears to be three sets of virtues commonly propounded within the Craft. Two sets, which are perhaps more common in writings, are, on the one hand, Brotherly Love, Relief, and Truth, each having, at least according to some, a direct relation with, on the other, the second set of Fraternity, Equality, and Liberty.

Wisdom, Strength and Beauty, however, appear more frequently in one form or another in *visual* form. In other words, these allegories are illustrated with symbols, and through their further exegesis we may come to slowly unveil their multi-layered, but also precise, meanings.

Specifically as *pillars* of Wisdom, Strength and Beauty, they also harkens to Kabbalistic works, and it is to this we shall now turn our attention to, at first without consideration of Freemasonic concern, and only later shall we begin to take steps to posit ways to reconcile the two in harmonious ways.

Kabbalah

Kabbalistic considerations have been influential within European culture since before the 15th century. Indeed, it was in part adopted and adapted by some in an attempt to convert Jews to Christianity, using the Trinitarian imagery found in some version of the Tree of Life to argue for the validity of a Trinitarian theology.

Here we are of course not concerned with this aspect, nor with the numerous forms the pattern of the Tree of Life takes (many of which non-pillar related). For the sake of liberating considerations to be more fluid rather than fixed, consider for a moment the emanations that make the Tree of Life as concentric circles, each enclosing and giving rise to ever denser manifestation *within* its own onion-like layer.

Such was a common enough rendition. What is here important as a first consideration is that there are ten successive emanation from the 'unmanifest', or, rather, to give it its Hebrew name, from the *Ein Sof* - without limit.

Whether this is equivalent to Aristotle's unmoved mover[3] is something that needs much further exploration. For our purposes, let's just take it that there is some parity between the concepts.

From this *Ein Sof* emanates ten successive contractions. It is also relatively simply to here imagine how this model reflects also the ancient view of the universe, with the Kingdom of the Earth at its very centre.

These successive emanations or *Sefirot* were at times also represented as fruits at the end of a Tree having its roots embedded within the spiritual domain:

It is but by a short series of variations that we arrive at some of the most common and popular versions of the Tree of Life. In each case, what is of unalterable significance is, on the one hand, that there are ten Sefirot (i.e., emanations)[4]; and on the other that these have their precise ordering, even when arranged in a manner that lacks apparent sequentiality.

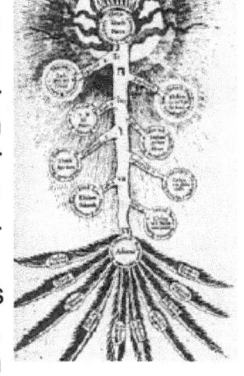

Of direct significance for our purposes are three specific *Sefirot*: the second, *Hockmah*; the fifth, *Geburah*; and the sixth *Tifaret*. These have meanings that are of course embedded very much within Hebrew, and their translated meanings do not have precisely the same scope or terrain as their English translations. In the case of *Geburah* and *Tifaret*, there are also different translations possible. Significantly, however, these can (and often are) rendered as, respectively, *Wisdom*, *Strength*, and *Beauty*.

---

[3] *Cf.* his *Physics* 3,2
[4] As the Sefer Yetzirah, possibly a circa 2nd century text, states "Ten Sefirot out of Nothingness: Ten and not nine, ten and not eleven".

Let's see how these are placed on the more common base of the Tree of Life diagrammes, that of Kircher:

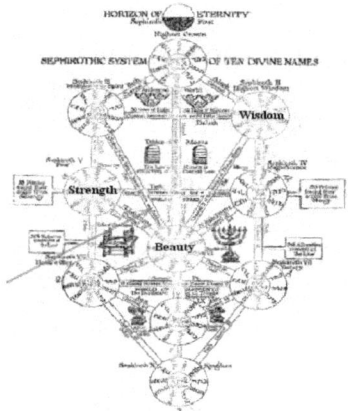

I have highlighted in red the pertinent *Sefirot*, each situated, instructively, upon one of three (hereon blued) columns or pillars. The green arrow indicates the same direction of view that one needs to assume to mimic the Harris tracing board earlier presented. The other tracing board would be viewed from exactly *below*, 'projecting' the lowest central *Sefirot* of Beauty to its pinnacle.

Let's have a closer look at all these things and begin to fuse them into a coherent syncretic whole.

Entering the Lodge room

When we penetrate within the doors of the Lodge opened in the first degree, amidst all the other emblems, symbols and furnishings, we are faced with inner stillness and silence except by instruction of the Master or the two Wardens.

These, in turn, have pillars and lights associated with them.

Reflecting on their combined responsibilities, they represent Wisdom, Strength and Beauty, bringing to mind that, as each also reflects the first[5] three degrees, we are lead to consider that the work consists in beautifying, strengthening, and the getting of wisdom.

---

[5] I am aware that many are of the view that there are only, and precisely, three degrees in Freemasonry. I simply note here that such remains, no matter how dominant and 'officially' pronounced, one amongst other views.

Looking at the tracing board[6], we note that the pillars, associated with the principal officers, have distinct working tools, and the Sun, Moon and Sacred Star (or all-seeing Eye) surmounts the pillars. As with the stair or ladder upon which are the three virtues of *Faith, Hope* and *Charity*, the luminaries in the sky are not physically within the Lodge room, reminding us that in active work, we transcend the limitations of the walls in which we may consider ourselves to otherwise be.

Observing the Tree of Life, we note that each pillar has not only one *Sefirah*, but others. It is each united with the others that form pillars, and so we ascend, with the aid of the plumb-rule, level and square, and the assistance of Faith, Hope, and Charity, towards building those pillars not built by hand. And on these we now turn, taking into consideration each pillar in turn, yet mindful that our ascent spirals, in that the foundations of each pillar needs to be worked before rising to successive levels.

The Pillars

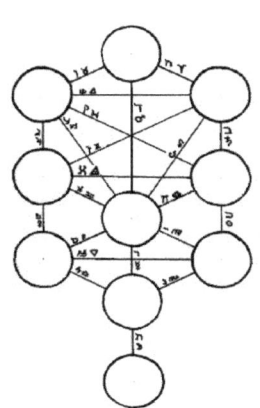

A friend of mine, both a former Grand Chaplain[7] and subsequently a Bishop, once described a meditation in which he saw - with the mind's eye - a pebble dropped into a water's surface. The concentric circular rippling that occurred was like the first representation of the Tree of Life I presented earlier. Hence, a hand came down and lifted the pebble, dressed in the gown of the water's surface, giving rise to a Kircher-like (here a Lurianic) version of the Tree of Life:

---

[6] Again, not all Lodges even have trestle or tracing boards.
[7] Lodges warranted under certain Grand Lodges have Chaplains and, in turn, the Grand Lodge a Grand Chaplain. Though the position need not be filled by a priest or other minister of a Church, it often is.

Let's consider each pillar in turn. First the central one of Beauty, then the left-hand of Strength, and finally the right-hand one of Wisdom. In that order, we are also first advancing on those emanations that we reach in their order of *ascent*. Whether the Master or a Warden is there connected I leave to the reader, simply asking that the earlier considerations as to the Floor Plan in use, and the relative placement of the three pillars (when three are used).

Beauty

Beauty, *Tifaret*, is the central golden globe here shown. It is often allied to the Sun.

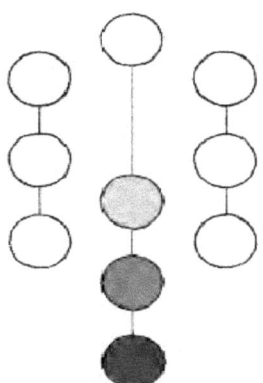

Somewhere (and I cannot recall the source), I once read that "in *Tifaret*, conflict is reconciled, and contradiction resolved".

Below it are, respectively, *Yesod* (Foundation) and *Malkut* (Kingdom). As these two are, respectively, often connected to the Moon and the Earth, we have here an ascent from Earth, to Moon, to Sun, to the Sun-beyond-the-Sun (alluded to in Plato's 'allegory of the Cave' in Book VII of his *Republic*[8]) as *Keter* (the Crown).

The lowest of the two require that we both keep our feet on the ground and that we build a solid foundation before ascending further. We have physical body, and life forces with which to work and direct. These provide initial work.

It is appropriate that the pillar is named by the central *Sefirah*, for the highest reminds one of Enoch: he 'walked with God, and was not'.[9]

---

[8] So here we have both Plato's concept of ultimate 'Good' and Aristotle's concept of the Unmoved Mover connecting to the highest of realms.
[9] Genesis 5:24

Strength

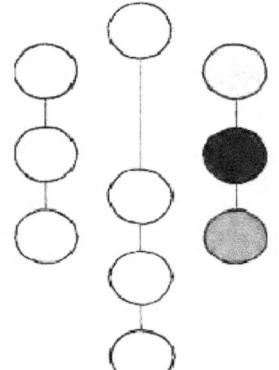

Strength, *Geburah*, is here the central red emanation. It's more common translation is 'severity', but even in Hebrew, it has another common name: *Pahad*, or 'fear' - as in '*Pahad* of the Lord is the beginning of Wisdom'.[10] It should be noted here that *Pahad* is better rendered by 'Awe', an aspect intimately connected to the concept of 'fear' that seems to have perished.

'Awe awakens in us the possibility of knowledge and wisdom' may here perhaps also be considered.

Strength is, of course, one of the cardinal virtues, and central to both Aristotelian and Platonic considerations of what makes a person Good or virtuous, and can lead to a desirable life. As strength, it is often connected with Mars.

Below *Geburah* is the emanation of Mercury, *Hod* or Glory. Combining these, I am lead to reflect on Goethe's exquisite 'Fairy Tale of the Green Snake and the Beautiful Lily'[11], in which a catechism presents itself:

"What is grander than gold?" inquired the King. "Light," replied the Snake. "What is more refreshing than light?" said he. "Speech"[12]

Above *Geburah* is *Binah*, Understanding. It has the vast emptiness of fecund space, a space filled with light, but as yet to give birth to object on which such light will be reflected.

---

[10] Psalm III:10. But note also Proverbs 1:7, where 'Knowledge' is used in lieu of 'Wisdom'.
[11] A 'fairy tale' for adults, or at the very least for his brothers in Freemasonry, if ever there was one!
[12] Sometimes translated as 'communication' – something very Mercurial.

Wisdom

Here it is the top *Sefirah*, that of *Hockmah* (Wisdom), that is indicated. It is the closest one can strive to the source of all other emanations.

It also points that all emanation, passing through this *Sefirah*, is imbued with Wisdom, even is layers obscure its glow.

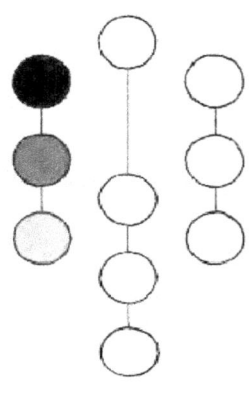

Below are *Hesed*, sometimes translated as Loving-kindness, but also the word used for 'covenant': a binding together of willing parties. Below that, at its foundation, sits *Netzah*, victory or reverberation, hinting that each of our acts, feelings and thoughts reverberate and have their own victories beyond the confines we may otherwise wish.

Three Pillars, or two?

And so we finish where we started. The pillars, whether as two or three, call to mind far more than mere 'lesser' lights!

Viewing the pillars Boaz and Jachin as the two extremes, we are asked to pass *between* them, reminding those who have taken to heart the study of the seven liberal hearts and sciences that it is the golden mean between extremes that reflects virtue. The extremes also remind us of the two pillars between which our life stands as its own third pillar - between the portals of birth and death."[13]

---

[13] R. Steiner also makes this connection between the two pillars and death, between which, he is claimed to have uttered "we have the time of our life" (obviously to its ambiguity in English). *Cf* Lecture 3, "The Twelve Senses, 20th June 1916, in *Toward Imagina*tion.

I am here reminded of the beautiful Masonic pillars that once adorned the sides of the doors of the Würzburg Cathedral (often referred to in various Freemasonic writings). Like Floor Plan A and the 18th century tracing board, passing through the pillars leads one to the inner sanctum whereby the third pillar is implied by the Master in the East - in the case of the Cathedral (and hence for the Christian), by Christ not only crucified, but in Ascension.

If we observe closely the 'knots' of these two pillars, they illustrate clearly that their respective foundation is two-fold: each pillar effectively has two bases, one standing on the ground; the other in the celestial realm. What 'binds' them together appears as inter-weavings - I would here say the inter-weavings of life's weavings itself.

And so, we are lead to consider how to best make that binding strong, beautiful and wisdom-filled by further considering the *Sefirot* or emanating spheres on the Tree of Life.

Whether two pillars are represented, or three, there is always an implied third element, each able to guide us in the consciousness of daylight as well as by the darkness visible in the spiritual light of night.

Select Bibliography

Aristotle   *Physics*
Nichomachean Ethics, Findlen, P. (ed.)

Athanasius Kircher, Routledge, 2004

Goethe, J. W. Von, *The Fairy Tale of the Green Snake and the Beautiful Lily*, online edition at:
http://wn.rsarchive.org/RelAuthors/GoetheJW/GreenSnake.html

Jones, B. E. *Freemasons' Guide and Compendium*, (rev. ed.) Harrap London, 1956

Kaplan, A.
> *The Bahir*, Samuel Weiser, 1979
> *Sefer Yetzirah*, (rev. ed.) Samuel Weiser, 1997

Plato, *Republic*

Steiner, R. *Toward Imagination*, [GA 169], Anthroposophic Press, 1990

THE TRACING BOARD[1]

By: Giorgio Rocchi

Some Brethren think that that the Tracing Board, or the Trestle Board, is superfluous, because it repeats architectonic and decorative elements which are already in the Temple.

In their opinion the Tracing Board was useful in ancient times, when Freemasons met in private houses or in taverns, so it remind them the tools of each degree; nowadays, however, it is completely useless. They think so because they are unaware of the main law which rules any symbol, be it sonorous, visual or otherwise figurative, that is, the relationship between the symbol and the relevant symbolized object, the latter being always superior to the former.

A symbol lies always at a lower stage in respect of the reality which it symbolizes, for it has to be perceived through human senses, while the same cannot happen for a metaphysical idea. Therefore, the Tracing Board's symbols allude to a super-human reality.

The manifold meanings of the same symbol have not to cheat the interpreter: each symbol has various meanings because it can be considered at various levels; this difference, however, is always reflecting an analogy's relationship.

We can therefore say that the Tracing Board does never reproduce the Temple's architectonic elements; if ever, the contrary is true, that is, man took elements out of the Tracing Board to decorate the Temple, as it has happened with regard to other traditional arts, whereby symbols became ornaments so to survive even if man does not understand them any longer.

Even admitting that the Tracing Board does not symbolize the Temple, but metaphysical realities, man could then

---

[1] *Rivista Massonica* n. 1 Gennaio 1973 – vol. LXIV – VIII della nuova serie – pp. 39-43

wonder whether these realities can be illustrated by the Temple's structures, so to make the Tracing Board superfluous. On this subject man can elaborate further considerations which however lead us to the same conclusion, that is, the need of the Tracing Board which cannot be substituted by anything else.

With regard to visual or figurative symbols we notice that some of them are traced when the rite starts and are deleted at the end. This is not only a precaution against profanes' curiosity, but rather the consequence of the close link existing between symbol and rite, so that the former has no ground to exist outside the latter.

This happens for many *yantras*, in Hindu tradition, and also for the Tracing Board, which was drawn on the sand or on the earth and then erased, in ancient times, while today man lays a picture on the floor and then withdraws it, when the Masonic works are over. Man cannot proceed in the same way with the whole Temple's furniture, at least easily and quickly.

Taking an example from magic ceremonies, man can say that the Tracing Board works like a condenser of subtle energies which, once attuned and amplified, should attract the *Shekina*, the spiritual influence.

"The kingdom of heaven suffereth violence"[2] means also that man can attract spiritual influences by means of certain techniques which are of essence in certain rituals.

In some magic ceremonies the sorcerer traces a circle which represents his will and acts as a condenser of subtle energies which shall protect him against the forces he will later evoke.

By tracing and erasing the circle, from time to time, the sorcerer expresses his will and makes the circle valuable and meaningful. Should he trace the circle once for ever, it would soon be "discharged", deprived of any effectiveness.

The Tracing Board works in the same manner. The Brethren's energies flow together in it. For this reason the

---

[2] Matthew 11:12

Tracing Board will not be lain immediately, but only after the works have ritually started, so to have enough time to attune energies.

There is another aspect to examine, that is, "the relationship of inversed analogy's law".

According to this law, the first in the principal order is the last and the smallest in the manifestation: "but many who are first will be last, and many who are last will be first".[3]

The main feature of this relationship consists in that, that the perspectives is actually upset when man moves from the physical plan to the metaphysical one.

So, at a material level the centre matches the inner point and is contained in the whole: centre of a circumference, a circle, a sphere. Pascal moved from this perspective when he stated that the space is like a sphere, the centre of which is everywhere while the circumference is nowhere.

At a metaphysical level, however, such a perspective is void, for the Centre, the Principle, wraps everything.

In Dante's Paradise the Empire, the central heaven, embraces all other heavens.

According to this viewpoint, man has to upset Pascal's statement, for the "centre" is nowhere, it being an atemporal and dimensionless entity, transcendent any physical reality.

Masonically, the same thought is valid for the geometric centre, from which a Master Mason cannot err.

In conclusion, the metaphysical realities that are envisaged in the Tracing Board contain the physical ones. Conversely, passing from the spiritual order to the material one, the lodge – which is symbol of the cosmos – wraps the Tracing Board, which symbolizes the centre, in its spatial dimension, though.

---

[3] Matthew 19:29-30

GODS IN LODGE

By: Piero Vitellaro Zuccarello

The Masonic temple, as a whole, is a symbol of the cosmos. The word "lodge" stems from Sanskrit *loka,* which means place, world, community, common practice: it is the place *par excellence*, the length of which is comprised between West and East, its width between North to South, its height between Nadir and Zenith".[1] The starred sky lays over the lodge; together with the sun, the moon and the zodiac, it completes the temple's astral symbolism.

Gods are still in it. Although the external Greek-roman polytheistic cult came to an end in as a result of Emperor Theodosius's edict, in 380 C. E., the intellectual principles, symbolized by the gods are still present in the Masonic temple. The esoteric researcher compares them with the monotheistic exotericism's angels and, going beyond the apparent duality, perceives various aspects of the unique divinity; nothing exterior to oneself, but rather interior states to be realized within.

On this subject, René Guénon wrote: "Actually, the states we are talking about differ from the human state more than any western philosopher could ever imagine, nevertheless, and regardless the beings who actually occupy them, they can be realized by any other, even by a human being in another state of the manifestation... We have already noticed that what man theologically says about angels can be repeated for the superior states of the being; likewise, in Middle-ages' astrological symbolism "heavens", that is planetary spheres and stars, not only represent those states, but also the initiatic degrees to which their realization corresponds; even more, in the Hindu tradition, Deva and Asuras symbolize the superior and inferior states, respectively, *vis-à-vis* the human state".[2]

---

[1] J. Boucher, *La Simbologia Massonica*, Atanòr p. 81
[2] R. Guénon, *The multiple states of the Being*, Sophia Perennis, Hillsdale

The Supreme Principle, which in Masonic terms man calls The Great Architect of the Universe and also Universal Man, is found in the equilateral triangle which is suspended over the Worshipful Master's chair. Inside it there is the Jewish *Tetragrammaton*, a *yod* or an "all seeing eye".

"The *Tetragrammaton* always occupies a central position, being expressly placed between the sun and the moon. From this it follows that the eye within this triangle should not be represented in the form of an ordinary left or right eye, since these are really the sun and the moon, corresponding respectively to the right and left eyes of 'Universal Man' insofar as the latter is identified with the 'macrocosm'. For the symbolism to be entirely correct, this eye must be a 'frontal' or 'central' eye, that is, a 'third eye', whose likeness to the *yod* is still more striking; and it is indeed this 'third eye' that 'sees all' in the perfect simultaneity of the eternal present."[3]

Various symbols represent as many principal attributes which are tied to the Greek-Roman myth, either directly or indirectly and to other traditions. Out of them, only three refer to the classic myth. They are the statues of Pallas, Venus and Heracles (or even Junos, as discussed below); and the other three, the sun, the moon and the starry heaven, refer to gods. Last, but not the least, let me recall another important god-symbol, Janus Bifrons (double-faced), which is not in the lodge but is in the Masonic calendar, Christianized as the two Saints John.

Janus

The Masonic feast of Saint John Evangelist fall on the 27th December, near to Winter Solstice, and that of Saint

---

NY p. 70

[3] From the point of view of 'triple time', the moon and the left eye correspond to the past, the sun and the right eye to the future, and the third eye to the present, that is, to the invisible 'instant' between past and future, that is a reflection of eternity in time. Cf. R. Guénon, "the all-seeing eye", in *Symbols of Sacred Science, Sophia Perennis*, Hillsdale NY

John Baptist on 24th June, the Summer Solstice. In those same periods *Collegia Fabrorum,* the Roman crafts, celebrated Janus.[4]

Janus is properly the *Door Man* who opens and closes the doors (*januæ*); with reference to the annual astronomical cycle these doors correspond to the Solstices. Indeed, Janus was the god of initiation; to him Romans dedicated the first month: *Januarius (January)*.

Janus is double-faced. On the one side, he looks at the past, on the other one, to the future. He holds a scepter in the right hand and a key in the left one, symbols, respectively, of "greater mysteries" and "lesser mysteries".[5] Worthy of note is his association with coins, since most Roman coins reproduced his picture. In ancient times monetization was a sacred art.[6] Janus is eventually believed to have introduced men to navigation's art, hence the nautical symbolism.

The Sun

In lodge, the sun's symbol is placed in correspondence with the Orator's chair. The sun's immutability makes it reflect the main cosmic immutability. While the moon changes itself through its phases, the sun arises, culminates and sets, being always equal to itself. It does not die at sun-set but descends "into the lower regions, into the kingdom of the dead", with a salvation's function, and resurrects the subsequent day.[7]

Among the various solar deities which man finds in different traditions, the Greek-Roman god Apollo is quite im-

---

[4] R. Guénon, *ibidem*, p. 235
[5] Nicola Turchi, *La religione di Roma Antica*, Cappelli
[6] The Latin word *moneta*, coin, stems from *Junos Moneta*, from the Latin verb *moneo*, to admonish (cf. also English "money"). The goddess admonished goldsmiths to work with a spiritual intent. [ED]. On this subject cf. R. Guénon, T*he reign of quantitiy and the signs of the times.* Chap. 16 *The Degeneration of Coinage*
[7] Mircea Eliade, *Patterns in comparative religions,* University of Nebraska Press, p. 136

portant for Freemasonry. "Apollo, in the Greeks' classic theology, represents the 'shining' sun, *fóibos*, which by its rays' power can treat and heal (*asclépios*); by his gleaming eye the god scans the occult and is, therefore, the divination's father, the oracles' god, manifest by his ministrations."[8] These features, together with those of legislator and interpreter of the law – according the myth he is at origin of Sparta's legislation, besides Lycurgus[9] – explain the tight connections of Apollo to the lodge's orator: this one is the custodian of both the Sacred Law and its relevant connection with the 'greater mysteries'.

Apollo-Sun symbolizes the immanent intellect: he orders chaos by killing Python, the monstrous cosmic serpent, then, at Delphi, he sets up the most important spiritual center in Greece. Before doing so, Apollo rode on the back of a swan – or on a swan-shaped chariot – to the land of the Hyperboreans, for the siege on the supreme spiritual center, after which he came back to found the Delphic spiritual center.

Apollo was sacred to the Pythagoreans, the initiatory organization which constitutes the oldest root of Freemasonry: the Pythagorean Abaris, Apollo's Hyperborean priest, traveled around the world sitting on a golden arrow, symbol of the immanent intellect.[10]

The Moon

If the Sun reflects the cosmic immutability, the Moon is surely symbol of the becoming and changing, given its continuous changes through its various phases.

We find this symbol associated with the Secretary's seat. The Secretary's initiatory function is tied to the Lodge's collective memory, which he has to create by writing the relevant minutes. Starting from this memory's cast man has to get at a new phase of business; the memory,

---

[8] Nicola Turchi, *La religione di Roma Antica*, Cappelli
[9] W. Guthrie, I *Greci e i loro dei,* Il Mulino, pp. 222-223
[10] W. Guthrie, *Ibidem*, p. 93 ss.

the relevant cast and the "passage" to a new shape refer to the lunar symbolism which exists, with a few of differences, in all traditions, symbolized by various lunar deities, be they either male or female, such as Persephone, Artemis-Seléne and the Vedic Chandra.

Mircea Eliade notes that "the oldest Indo-Aryan root connected with heavenly bodies is the one that means "moon": it is the root *me*, which in Sanskrit becomes *mami*, "I measure". The moon, by its regularity of appearance through its various phases becomes the universal measuring gauge. All the words relating to the moon in the Indo-European languages come from that root.

Time as governed and measured by the phases of the moon might be called 'living' time. It is bound up with the reality of life and nature, rain and the tides, the time of sowing, the menstrual cycle. A whole series of phenomena belonging to totally different 'cosmic levels' are ordered according to the rhythms of the moon or are under its their influence.[11]

The root *me* further expands into the Sanskrit 'man', the main meaning of which is "to think" and from which stem the English and German terms "moon" and "Mond", respectively.

From the same root stem both the Latin *mens* and the Sanskrit *manas*, which refer to mind. This etymological research lets us establish a relationship between the measure, to be intended mainly as measure of time, and the mental activity, comprising the discursive and analytical thought, on the one hand, and the moon, which is seemingly set against the sun, symbol of the intuitive and integrative mind. Actually, man solves such an opposition through the triangle. The ternary triangle-sun-moon is tightly linked to Kabbalah's Sephirot Kether, Hokmah and Binah.

The moon is a symbol intimately linked to individual functions: to the thought which goes through temporality,

---

[11] M. Eliade, *Patterns in comparative religions*, University of Nebraska Press, p. 154

imaginative forms and memory. Other symbols are linked to the moon: the spiral, the serpent, the "inferior waters" of any formal potentialities. They are all symbols of the cyclic manifestation.

According to Hindu tradition, after his earthly death, a man can walk two paths: the ignorant, once arrived at the moon, which is the deposit of the cosmic memory, will stop there and therefore will fall again into the formal status, taking a new individual form. They walk on "the fathers' way" (*pitriyana*). Conversely, the initiates will go beyond the moon's sphere, arriving at the supra-formal states and therefore will walk on "the gods' way" (*devayana*). In this last case the moon appears as "immortality's door"; the moon's Vedic god Chandra - closely linked to Soma, the immortality's beverage - is the relevant symbol.[12]

"As to the death we die, one death reduces man from three factors to two and another reduces him from two to one; and the former takes place in the earth that belongs to Demeter (wherefore "to make an end" is called "to render one's life to her" and Athenians used in olden times to call the dead "Demetrians"), the latter in the moon that belongs to Persephone, and associated with the former is Hermes the terrestrial, with the latter Hermes the celestial. While the goddess here dissociates the soul from the body swiftly and violently, Persephone gently and by slow degrees detaches the mind from the soul and has therefore been called "single-born" because the best part of man is "born single" when separated off by her. Each of the two separations naturally occurs in this fashion: All soul, whether without mind or with it, when it has issued from the body is destined to wander in the region between earth and moon but not for an equal time."[13]

While ambitious and egotistical men run toward Earth, initiates are attracted by the Sun, to the essence which corresponds the intellect. Birth happens in the inversed man-

---

[12] R. Guénon, *L'uomo ed il suo divenire secondo il Vedanta*, cap. 2
[13] Plutarch, *De facie in orbe lunæ*, chap. 28 p199-p201

ner: "earth furnishes the body, the moon the soul, and the sun furnishes mind to man for the purpose of his generation even as it furnishes light to the moon herself."[14]

The Starry Heaven

A picture of the starry heaven is on the lodge's ceiling. Both the Greek god Ouranos and – even better – his Vedic equivalent Varuna, are lords of the starry heaven. Their names stem from the same Indo-European root; *var*, to cover. In Masonic rituals the Tyler represent these two gods by acting to separate the sacred space from the profane one.

The *Atharvaveda* portrays Varuna as omniscient, catching liars in his snares. The stars are his thousand-eyed spies, watching every movement of men. He his omniscient and omnipotent, able to tie men to himself through subtle and mysterious bonds: "and Varuna's nets are to be feared for they are bonds which paralyze and exhaust".[15]

Varuna is king, not by himself (svaraj, like Indra) but samraj, universal king. That is to say, power is his by right because his very nature; this power enables him to act through 'magic', through the 'power of the mind', through 'knowledge'.[16] Varuna is also god of the sky and rain, therefore he is associated to waters which, in this case, are not symbol of formal possibilities, as in the lunar symbolism, but of supra-formal manifestation, since they convey to earth heavenly spiritual influences.[17]

Pallas, Venus, and Heracles

The General Statutes of Scottish Freemasonry, released at Naples in 1820, declare that: *"The statues of Pal-*

---

[14] *ibidem*, p.199
[15] M. Eliade, *ibidem*, p. 69
[16] M. Eliade, *ibidem*, p. 71
[17] R. Guénon, *Symbols of Sacred Science*, chap 60 p. 353. Cf. also *Idem, L'uomo ed il suo divenire secondo il Vedanta*, and *The multiple states of Being*.

las, Heracles and Venus, symbolizing wisdom, strength and beauty, respectively, are to be seen in the Masonic temple."
According to Bro. René Guénon: *"... the 'Divine Aspects' are each regarded as being endowed with a power or energy of their own, called Shakti, which is represented symbolically under a feminine form: the Shakti of Brahma is Saraswati, that of Vishnu is Lakshmi, and that of Shiva is Parvati."*[18]

Much to our surprise, we find out that Sarasvati, Vedas' mother, creator of Sanskrit language, patroness of arts and sciences, owns the same wisdom's attributes as goddess Pallas,[19] Lakshmi is the Hindu Aphrodite who is born out of the sea, as well as Venus.[20]

With regard to Heracles, we note that his name means 'Hera's glory'; actually under Hera's persecution Heracles fulfills his tasks till his sacrificial death and transfiguration. Giovanni de Castro replaces Heracles with Junos, thus obtaining a triad which is compound by Junos, or power; Pallas, or wisdom and Venus, or beauty.[21] It is the same triad as the one of the 'Judgment of Paris', which provoked the war of Troy.

Junos-Hera is the goddess of weddings and births who also displays destructive aspects, by driving Heracles to madness.[22] Shiva's shakti, Parvati, has lovely and motherly attributes, but she is also Durga, the warrior, who cannot be approached, as well as Kali, "the Black", who wears a chain of skulls.[23]

On the other hand, Shiva, husband of Shiva, creates and destroys the manifestation, transforming it, that is, going beyond the form. These features link him to the highest and most delicate aspects of any initiatic realization and associate him to Dionysus, the Greek-Asian god who pre-

---

[18] *L'uomo ed il suo divenire secondo il Vedanta,* Adelphi, p. 158
[19] A. Morretta, *Miti indiani,* p. 216
[20] *Ibidem,* p. 219
[21] A. Reghini, *Il manuale dell'apprendista libero muratore,* p. 49
[22] R. Graves, *I miti greci*
[23] A. Morretta, *ibidem* p. 232-234

sides over the overwhelming of human limits. Dionysus, as god of any transcending action, is seemingly opposite to Apollo, god of the limit, but both gods complete each other at a superior unitarian level. For this reason they are present at Delphi.

Conclusions

Freemasonry maintained many elements of a symbolic heritage, which is ancient and noble, indeed. We therefore conclude by saying that, notwithstanding the present decadence, Freemasonry is still an initiatory experience very close to the Unique Tradition of the Origins.

THE BLAZING STAR

By Giovanni Lombardo

In the Masonic temple, above the Worshipful Master's throne, there is the blazing star. Man may also call it *pentalfa*, five *alfa*, that is, five principles, because it adds intelligence to the traditional four existing ones – earth, water, air and fire.[1]

Its origin is Pythagorean, if man will find it in the Hebrew speculation, too. Its meaning is complex: it includes the numbers 2, 3 and 5. In the centre there is a pentagon, which symbolizes the union between 3, the masculine principle, and 2, the feminine one.

In the Pythagorean school pupils had to trace the star all in one movement, so to stress the idea of the restored oneness.

The letter G is in the centre. "G" stands for God, but also for Geometry, the divine science which regulates the cosmic harmony. However some people interpret it as *Gnòsis*, the heuristic knowledge of the supreme truth which initiates can attain walking the inner path.

In Freemasonry the blazing star symbolizes the central fire, man's inner centre from which stems the true light, the divine science.

The fifth Tarot Atout of the Major Arcanes is the Hierophant, an old, wise man who joins earth and heaven. Astrologically, it is associated to Aries, for it is pushing men to search for light and love. In Latin, the pope is said *pontifex*, *pontem facere*, that is, to cast a bridge from earth to heaven.

The blazing star is therefore the sacred fire of the divine spirit which is embodied into humankind. It symbolizes the

---

[1] *Alfa* is the first letter of the Greek alphabet.

inner enlightenment, that is, intuition, which guides any initiate who is aware to be a microcosm, so having a principle of order, harmony and perfection within himself.

Alchemists thought the blazing staring expressed the celestial *quinta essentia* and therefore they called it "the philosophical child". It is another way to hint at the embodied divinity, the conscience's principle.

The blazing star is also Christ's emblem. It guided the Magi towards Bethlehem, showing the way not only geographically, but rather allegorically: the divine birth matches the initiatory rebirth.

God devolved upon Adam the following message: "and God said, let us make man in our image, after our likeness".[2] The divine principle was in Adam's body; the spirit was within him. Jesus relaunched this message universally: "the word became flesh and made his dwelling among us."[3]

Each human being is therefore able to meet the Father, becoming one into One. The "image" and the "likeness" can become reality within everybody's reach, through a method which freemasonry is still keeping and which allows initiates to obtain the esoteric knowledge.

---

[2] Genesis 1:26
[3] John 1:14

THE POINT WITHIN THE CIRCLE

By: Bruce Nevin

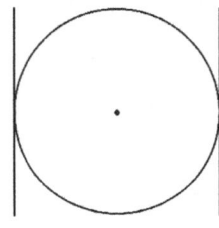

One of the emblems in every regular and well-furnished Lodge is a point at the center of a circle, embordered by two perpendicular parallel lines. The point, we are told, represents an individual Brother, and the circle the boundary line of his duty.

On the face of it, this alludes to the injunction to circumscribe our desires and keep our passions within due bounds. On first consideration, it seems that the circle represents an externally imposed constraint, defined by the precepts of the holy Saints John of Jerusalem[1] together with those articulated in the Book of Holy Scripture. In this centripetal interpretation, the circle represents an externally imposed boundary pressing in from the outside toward the center so as to constrain the free expression of the individual within due bounds. This is consistent with the, alas, common misconception that human nature is fundamentally depraved, and must be constrained if social life is to be made possible.

This emblematic image of the point within the circle has far more to tell us, however. To begin, consider that the Feast of Saint John the Evangelist is (or was originally) at the Winter Solstice, and that of Saint John the Baptist at the Summer Solstice. From this, we directly deduce that the perpendicular line on the south side of the circle represents Saint John the Evangelist, the sun being at its farthest southerly declination at the Winter Solstice, and the line on the north correspondingly represents Saint John the Baptist, the sun at that time shining its rays upon us from an angle

---

[1] In 1812, fearful of charges of sectarianism, the United Grand Lodge of England changed this from the Holy Saints John to Moses and Solomon, but traditions in e.g. the United States were not affected by this.

as far to the north as it ever attains during the year. This suggests a perspective in which the circle represents the annual circuit of seasons. At the top of the circle is the Vernal Equinox, associated with Easter, Passover, and the Light in the East, represented by the Book of Holy Scripture. At the bottom of the circle in the West is the Autumnal Equinox, where the work of the Masonic year begins.

Or again, thinking of the solstices from that larger astronomical perspective so familiar to Preston and other learned 18th century Brethren, the circle represents the orbit of the earth about the sun. At the summer solstice, the north pole points directly toward the sun, which consequently appears highest overhead at noonday, and the north part of the Temple is darkest. At the Winter Solstice, it is the south pole that leans directly toward the sun, and the north pole away from it, so that the sun at its meridian height is able to "dart its ray" through a window or under a lintel into the northerly recesses of a building as far as ever it can during the year. At Jerusalem, the sun is not sufficiently low in the southern sky even at midwinter to have been able to illuminate the north part of King Solomon's Temple, but as we travel northward around the curvature of the earth, the midwinter sun appears progressively lower in the sky until, at the arctic circle, the winter sun is actually below the horizon at midday. At the equinoxes, the polar axis of the earth tilts at right angles to the sun. In the Spring, the north pole is turning progressively toward the sun, and at the Fall equinox it is turning progressively away. The solstices and equinoxes together divide the circle into four equal parts.

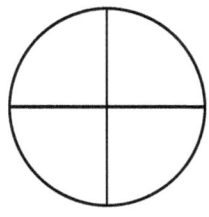

The sun at the center of our solar system is the source of energy that drives all living processes on our planet. Its unstinting expression of light and life is obviously not circumscribed by the orbit of the earth. It is the earth, rather, which in its orbit maintains just that distance from the sun at which there is sufficient irradiation, neither too much nor too little. Closer, and earth would be a barren desert; much farther, and ice ages would prevail without possibility of warming. This suggests a symbolism, not of constraint within a confining boundary, but rather of a median path, neither too much restraint nor too strong a projection away from the center.

The connection of the astronomical circle with the individual brother is that the sun, symbolically, has ever been associated with the heart of man, and with the central purpose of one's life, which must be felt out by trial and error in a process of refining the expression of one's heart's desire.

There is a dynamic relationship, then, between the centripetal and centrifugal aspects of this symbolism of a point within a circle, which may be illustrated by a practical consideration of our obligation. We are enjoined to help poor and distressed brethren and their families—but they must ask us for our help, we must find them worthy, and our assistance should do no injury to ourselves or our own families. We are obligated to answer all due signs and regular summonses from our Lodge—if within the length of our cable-tow. Just as one may use a piece of string and a pencil to draw a circle, the cable-tow circumscribes the extent of our capacity.

All of the ritual of the Lodge is centered on the altar, which we circumambulate in a clockwise direction. We call it clockwise because that is the direction that the hands of clocks move. Clocks run clockwise because that is the direction that the shadow of the gnomon moves on the face of a sundial, which mechanical clocks were made to imitate. The shadow moves clockwise because the sun rises in the east, transits through the southern sky, and sets in the west, casting shadows first to the west, then northward, and at sunset towards the east.[2] Together, the brightness of the sun and

---

[2] As is customary, we are ignoring the adjustments that are necessary in the southern hemisphere.

the darkness of the shadow, in their daily dance of polar opposites, describe a complete circle of clockwise motion, and indeed the motion of the shadow during the day foretells the returning passage of the sun through the north during the night, hidden from us by the bulk of the earth beneath our feet.

Our circumambulations of the altar are bounded on the north and south by the two parallel sidelines of the brethren duly assembled in a lodge. The Book of Holy Scripture, however, rests upon the altar in the center, together with the two other Great Lights of the lodge. Like the sun in the solar system, these are an outward representation of that source of life-giving light which resides in the heart of each brother. Recall the suggestive paradox of Saint Augustine, that God is like a circle whose center is everywhere and whose circumference is nowhere. The life and light of the Supreme Being indwells in each living heart. Each of us is a center of expression for that same Divine Presence of the Supreme Architect of the Universe. For each particular center of expression, there are certain restraints, on the one hand those natural limitations of expression which change and evolve through our growth in wisdom and understanding, and on the other hand those due restraints of courtesy, mutual consideration, empathy, and brotherly love which bind us in a greater whole.

What is a center? It cannot be comprehended except in reference to that which is not the center. The understanding or comprehension of a center as such is therefore inherently dualistic, even as the notion of a center affirms the unity of a central point. The unity is in the center, the pairs of opposites around the periphery. Often, we do not realize what and where the center is until we have gone away from it, explored the periphery to get our bearings, as it were, and returned. This is why it is necessary for the young to break out on their own, even to rebel against authority. While we are learning, authoritative rules and commandments prescribe how we should act. In order to grow in real understanding it may seem necessary that we test these prescriptive rules experientially by trial and error. As we grow in wisdom, we recognize that these rules are not after all prescriptions of how we should be; rather, they are descriptions of how we shall be when we ripen as centers of expression of that inner light. When we are young, we may feel uncertain of our identity and our worth in the world. This may lead us to live either in reaction against authority imposed upon us, or in conformity with a chosen authority of one sort or another, even perhaps what our elders consider to be a cult, subservience to which we paradoxically assert as the expression of our own free will. With maturity, as we outgrow this reactive need to defend our individuality, we are able to return to the center, and, recognizing it at last, we may find peace in what is truly our own unique contribution to the world. In the Rosicrucian grades of initiation, the very highest grade is *Ipsissimus*, a Latin word which may be translated "he who is most himself."

To define a center is to single it out. Conversely, to be singled out, distinguished from all else around, is to be defined as a center.

For example, in psychological terms, having a point of view defines a center to which all things in one's perceptual universe are related.

We apprehend things in terms of our point of view on pairs of opposites. Is it large or small? Hot or cold? Soft or hard? Fast or slow? Easy or difficult? Beautiful or ugly? Attractive or repulsive? Harmful or beneficial? And so on. As we identify our ego with a point of view, we project our perceptions of the world from that point of view outward. We forget that they are *our* perceptions from a subjective point of view, and imagine that they are the genuine objective properties of the world. Needless to say, not everyone has the same point of view.

Sacred writings of the Orient speak of pairs of opposites in the realm of name and form (*nama-rupa*), as indeed do the Mystery traditions in the West. What are these pairs of opposites? In truth, a polarity or contrast is a graduated scale of some perceptual property from one extreme to the other. Light and dark are but degrees of brightness of the light. Hot/cold, soft/hard, fast/slow, easy/difficult, beautiful/ugly, each of these polarities subsists in many degrees between one extreme and the other. Love and hatred are extremes of the same emotion, with degrees of liking and dislike between. Our point of view, expressed as a preference or demand, defines a center on a graduated scale. That center, the preferred value from our point of view, divides one end of the scale from the other, creating an opposition or polarity where in fact there is but one single property perceived in varying degrees. Having a preference creates an opposition between the two extremities of that which is not preferred. So it is that the third Patriarch of Ch'an Buddhism in China (which later developed into Zen in Japan) said "The Great Way (*mahayana*) is not difficult for those who make no demands. Make the smallest distinction, however, for or against, and Heaven and Earth are set infinitely apart."

Wielding the trowel to spread the cement of brotherly love often requires skillful navigation through the sea of pairs of opposites. When Brethren have different preferences or demands, the mental atmosphere becomes clouded and confusing, and the emotional waters are choppy and strewn with hidden hazards. Small differences become magnified as each advocate tries to pull the other towards what he perceives as the proper center. To pull someone toward a goal, you must lean away from the goal in the opposite direction, and perhaps even change your position to stand beyond the goal. It is even possible that "winning" may itself become the goal, with the risk of establishing a result that is no center at all for anyone.

Geometrically, a center is a single point without dimension, but this simplest of the geometrical figures cannot represent a center by itself. This is because a point without dimension cannot be discerned, it can only be defined in relative terms. Cartesian coordinates define a point in a graph, just as latitude and longitude define a point on the earth's surface. Because a center is an indivisible point, and a point is a figure without dimension, it can be recognized as a center only relative to that which is not the center.

That which is on one side of the center must be equal to that which is on the other side. This "not-center" stuff is symmetrically arranged around the center in pairs of opposites; if it were not so, the center would then be off-center, and therefore no center at all. In other words, if that which is on one side is not equal to that which is on the other, the center is elsewhere. The notion of center therefore entails symmetry and balance.

The simplest geometric representation of center vs. not-center is one line bisected by another. But this bisecting line must also be centered on the first, that is, each line must bisect the other. Otherwise, the point of bisection is not in the center of the whole figure.

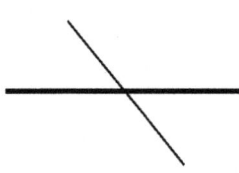

A simple archetype of the center is therefore the equal-armed cross. This figure has from time immemorial been emblematic of the intersection of positive and negative, male and female, yang and yin, as a creative, generative center of expression. The equal-armed cross divides the space around the center into four parts. Proper symmetry around the center requires that these four parts be equal, and for this reason the bisecting line must also be perpendicular to the other. This is a reason that we are concerned with horizontals and perpendiculars, and with the fourth part of a circle or the angle of ninety degrees.

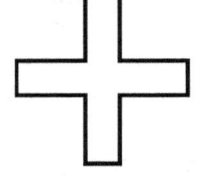

By careful inquiry into a controversy we can identify its terms. In any conflict, there is some perception that is preferred or demanded in one state, and simultaneously preferred or demanded in a different state. It can't be in both states at once. The room can be warmer or it can be cooler, but it can't be both warmer and cooler at the same time.

The ritual can be correct or the ritualist can be lenient, but not both at the same time.

A conflict cannot really be resolved head-on by taking sides, or by demanding an artificial compromise that neither party wants. Remember that the two preferences are separate points along a line of variation. Each party wants their preferred value to be the center. The path to resolution is at right angles to the conflict, as it were, by enquiring with each party why they have that preference. What is behind it? What purpose does it serve? When we step away from the particular demands that have got polarized in conflict, and go up a level to ask for the motivation, the larger or higher purpose for that preference, we begin talking about matters that are not in themselves in conflict, values on which we, in fact, are very likely to agree. The means that the antagonists have chosen for accomplishing those higher ends may be in conflict, but when we turn our attention to those higher purposes for which this bone of contention would be the means, the heat is off, and magical things can happen. Alternative means may become apparent. (Offer the chilly brother a jacket. Or perhaps the warm brother realizes he doesn't need that vest under his jacket. Or one may change his seat away from, or toward, a drafty spot.) More subtly, one preference may surprisingly dwindle in importance. More subtly yet, a point of view is not limited to a single preference, and we often find that some other intersecting preference is really much more important. Sometimes, at a higher level of motivations, the conflict simply dissolves, and no one quite knows how or why, or needs to know. This is the use of consciousness, represented traditionally by mercury, the universal solvent, to dissolve the bone of contention. If the cross of conflict be laid out on a plane surface, consciousness moves that crux vertically in the third dimension.

In an equal-armed cross, there are but two polarities. In a hexagon, a figure with six corners and six sides, there are three polarities crossing the center. In a circle, the number of pairs of opposites is infinite. For a point to be in the center, it must be equidistant from the extremities of the space in all directions around the center.

These considerations naturally lead us again to the image of a circle with a central point. In three dimensions, it leads us to a sphere. In the circle of the earth's orbit, the circle of the seasons, the summer solstice begins the descending half of the year, descending from the full expansion of light through the harvest season to the dark days of winter. Long before the Church subsumed them as the feast days of the Saints John, these have been sacred days in all times and places historic and prehistoric, and some have argued that our Masonic tradition here is a heritage from Druidic and other pre-Christian sources. Saint John the Baptist spoke strongly to the hearts of men, saying "Repent, for the Kingdom of God is at hand," and enjoining them to purity of heart and uprightness of life to make themselves fit citizens thereof. We cannot but be reminded of the symbolism of the lambskin, by which "we are continually reminded of that purity of life and conduct so essentially necessary to his gaining admission into the Celestial Lodge above, where the Supreme Architect of the Universe presides." The lambskin replaced a baptism with water that is found in early rituals, which was struck because, in ignorance, it was presumed to be an imitation of the Christian sacrament. John the Baptist remained faithful to his teaching of righteousness even to his execution by Herod, reminding us of Hiram Abiff.

The winter solstice begins the ascending half of the year, with the seed of reincarnated light planted in deepest darkness growing towards its fullness. Saint John the Evangelist spoke with equal fire and eloquence of the Light of the Logos, the creative Word of the Supreme Architect, coming into the world. We cannot but be reminded of the importance of the Word and the Light in our ritual. He was a follower of John the Baptist before he was made an Apostle. The Book of Revelation presents mysteries in symbol and allegory which we may assume were elucidated by instruction from mouth to ear, reminding us of these aspects of our ritual. His great and abiding lesson is to love one another. John the Evangelist concluded in learning and eloquence what Saint John the Baptist had begun in zeal, completing two parallel lines.

The emphasis that the two Saints John are "of Jerusalem" is suggestive. One of the accusations against the Templars was that they were followers of the Gnostic theology stemming from Saint John the Evangelist in the Church of Jerusalem, subsequently scattered in diaspora to other points in the Middle East, rather than the Roman Catholic interpretations of Saints Peter and Paul.

There are two pairs of opposites in a cross, three in a hexagon, but an infinite number in a circle or sphere of influence. As we grow in maturity to occupy the boundary line of our duty fully, life becomes an inexhaustible parade of preferences, rather than an addictive demand for particular stations on the scale between a few familiar pairs of opposites. To everything there is a season, and a time for every purpose under heaven. A person so ripened in wisdom is singularly equipped to be a peacemaker, spreading the cement of brotherly love.

This sheds light, too, on the injunction to keep our passions within due bounds. The passions of conflict are not present at the still center, they arise at the periphery, where we engage with one another. In youth, we strive to be independent. As we mature, we learn to be autonomous. Independence is a delusion. No man is an island. Autonomy is mastery of your boundaries, maintaining good interfaces with those around you.

Peace is not the absence of conflict. Conflict is a natural and inevitable consequence of living in one another's company as autonomous centers of expression. Conflict is not going away. It is unavoidable that we should on occasion find ourselves relying upon the same means to accomplish our different aims, I requiring those means in one state, you in another. This happens all the time, and we routinely negotiate an amicable resolution. We approach the same doorway from opposite sides. "Oh, excuse me!" says one, and "Thanks!" says the other, or "No, after you." Or perhaps both turn sideways and slip through the same opening cooperatively on their respective missions. Such are the ordinary skills of living that pass without notice until and unless there is some lapse in awareness or courtesy. So, no, peace is not the absence of conflict, it is the skillful resolving of conflicts as they arise. This is why peace will never be instituted by treaties or laws alone. It is a matter rather of more and more of us learning to be skillful peacemakers. In this we see also the truth of the saying "Blessed are the peacemakers, for they shall find peace," for the same skill at resolving conflicts among people resolves conflicts within ourselves, by raising our attention above the terms of conflict to the higher-level ends for which they are but means.

Disclosed now also is a deeper and richer understanding of the place of the individual brother within the circle comprising infinite pairs of opposites. The circle of a brother's duty is the extension of his influence and his responsibility to that just mean between centrifugal expression and centripetal restraint which truly articulates the utterly fulfilled peace of the divine spark in the stillness of the Holy of Holies within his heart. And as "deep calls unto deep" so does that free expression from within evoke awareness of the same divine Presence within the heart of each of his brethren, from which perspective no conflict is irresolvable. This is the true cement that is the foundation and support of civil society, and the guarantor of our Craft into the future as a vital leaven in the world.

WHAT IS AN EGREGORE?

By: R. Theron Dunn

Before starting, the author would like to express thanks to Wr. Giovanni Lombardo for his assistance in defining and bringing this article to the readers.

If you have never heard of the term "egregore", join the crowd. Many people have never heard the word, and until recently, that crowd included the author. A year ago, while posting on The Lodgeroom US, a fervent anti-Masonic... a poster, with the initials "T.S.", tossed out an unsupported and off topic slander to the effect that we masons should go back to working on evoking our egregore in lodge.

At the time, the author was stunned, never before having heard the word. A quick internet search revealed nothing, and not having any information on the subject, a research project was born, and thence this paper.

At the time, very little was available, though that has changed recently. One of the problems is that egregore is spelled two different ways, with a "E" at the end, and without. This made is difficult at first to find information.

So, what is an egregore, and how does it relate to Freemasonry?

Let start with a simple explanation of what an egregore is, or is reputed to be, and then move on from there. On this subject, there are various opinions, especially among "occultists" who seem to be the primary authors on the nature of the egregore. Following are the four primary occultist definitions:

An energized astral form produced consciously or unconsciously by human agency. In particular, (a) a strongly characterized form, usually an archetypal image, produced by the imaginative and emotional energies of a religious or magical group collectively, or (b) an astral shape of any kind, deliberately formulated by a magician to carry a specific force.[1]

...from a Greek word meaning "watcher." A thought-form created by will and visualization. A group egregore is the distinctive energy of a specific group of magicians who are working together, creating and building the same thought-form or energy-form.[2]

Any symbolic pattern that has served as a focus for human emotion and energy will build up an egregore of its own over time, and the more energy that is put into such a pattern, the more potent the egregore that will form around it. The gods and goddesses of every religion, past and present, are at the centers of vast egregore charged with specific kinds of power. This power is defined by, and contacted through, the traditional symbolism of the deity in question.[3]

An egregore is an angel, sometimes called watcher; in Hebrew the word is ir, and the concept appears in The Book of Enoch.... Thus, Irim, the city of the Nephilim is again linked with the Book of Enoch, since the Nephilim, according to that Book, were the sons of the Irim (the egregores.)....Although the Irim, the egregores, are angels on both sides of the camp - fallen angels as well as faithful ones.[4]

René Guénon, a prolific writer on Masonic philosophy offers the following: "First of all, we must point out that we have never used the word 'egregore' to designate what could properly be called a 'collective entity'; the reason for this is that the term is wholly untraditional and only represents one of the fantasies of modern occultist language.

---

[1] *Planetary Magick*, Denning & Phillips, (Llewellyn Publications)
[2] Golden Dawn Glossary
http://www.thelemicgnosticism.org/aa/contacts.htm
[3] John Michael Greer, from: *Inside a Magical Lodge*
[4] Egregore by L.S. Bernstein, http://www.crcsite.org/egregor.htm

The first person to use it (egregore) this way was Eliphas Levy, and if our memory is exact, it was he who, to justify this meaning gave it the improbable Latin etymology, deriving it from *grex*, 'flock', whereas the word is purely Greek and has never signified anything more than watcher."[5]

It appears therefore that, according to Guénon an egregore is a manifestation of psychic energy, as opposed to a spiritual force as the occultists would define it. Now that the author has completely confused you, let us proceed to dissect what we have as "definitions" to see if we can come to an understanding of the egregore, and its "place" in Freemasonry.

Of the definitions offered, that of Guénon seems to be the one that actually relates to masonry, while the others relate to religious/occult faith. The egregore is a psychic entity, existing between the material and the spiritual, in contact with both. It is the creation of the psychic will of the members of a group, and exists as a connection to the divine.

As we work rituals, the focused mental energy creates and invokes the egregore to fulfill the need of the group. An egregore is not a magical creature, it is not self aware, and is not a *Djin*, to carry out wishes. The egregore serves as a conduit, a nexus, to connect the group that created/invoked it to the spiritual.

Some egregores are temporary, while some, like the egregore of a lodge, a church, or a country, are the result of the continuous will that creates them, and this will also sustains them. The egregore of Freemasonry has existed for centuries, and is the result of the focused will to connect with the spiritual from millions of men.

An egregore is the psychic "entity". All members of a group, whether it is a club, your family, your lodge, a faith, a political party, a country, or even a single person, are united with the egregore of that group through a psychic connec-

---

[5] *Spiritual Influences and Egregores* by René Guénon, in *Initiation and Spiritual Realization, Sophia Perennis,* Hillsdale, N. Y. p37, paragraph 2

tion. As a result, and given the nature of society, we are often included in the sphere of several egregores at once.

The strength and ability of the egregore to aid and assist the members of the group grows over time and through numbers, by drawing support from the members constituting it and through their repeated actions maintain its power. The egregore, in turn, invokes the immaterial and raises us from the material, connecting us to the subtle worlds.

Where the intent is positive and spiritual, the effect of the egregore consists in conveying spirituality to the members as in the initiatic process of the lodge. The intent is to divest the candidate of the profane and connect him to the spiritual, and for most masons, that effect is felt and received most profoundly. To the contrary, in the case of other groups, especially the counter-initiatic ones – which adopt rites and symbols to attain profane or negative goals – the egregore can be quite destructive to the lives and spirits of those members.[6]

Each individual who is involved in a group is influenced by these egregores. For those that reach for a spiritual connection, the egregore assists and facilitates that connection. This process is unconscious, but is intensified through the initiatic process, which is designed to open the mind to the spiritual through the egregore.

A symbolic representation of this may be had in the examination of the Star of David, an emblem of the divine. The top triangle points the heavens, and to the spirit. The bottom triangle points down, to the material and profane. United, they form a new entity, the six-pointed star that represents the unity of the two, from material to the spirit, connection to the divine.

An example of this we are familiar with in Freemasonry is the Compasses and Square. The compass represents the male, the spiritual energy, while the square represents

---

[6] So it was in some Nazi esoteric groups, such as Thule or Vril. Also http://www.harare.unesco.org/hivaids/webfiles/Electronic%20Versions/malawi%20lifeskills.doc

the material. The compasses enclose and define the spiritual, as in the point within a circle, while the square defines the mortal, the material world. United, these two symbols, like the triangles, which form the Star of David, an emblem the represents the divine, so, too, does the square and compasses united, represent the divine, as is shown by the letter G in the middle.

So, the nature of the egregore has been known since time immemorial, as shown above. Its function is that of a guide, and intercessory, to conduct the group members to the spirit and connect them with it. Some groups are connected more powerfully from the profane and mortal side to the spiritual than others, some less so, but to each group according to its intent. As with all things, it is the intent that matters, not the form.

Guénon goes on to state, in reference to the egregore's influence: Man has, however, to point out that the Egregore "can never transcend the individual domain since, in the final analysis, it is only a resultant of the component individualities, nor, consequently, can it go beyond the psychic order; now all that is, only psychic can have no effective and direct relationship with initiation since this latter consists essentially in the transmission of a spiritual influence meant to produce effects of a similar spiritual order, thus transcendent with respect to the individuality, whence one obviously must conclude that whatever is able to render effective the initially virtual action of this influence, must itself necessarily have a supra-individual and thus, if one may put it so, a supra-collective character."[7]

In a lodge of Freemasons, the egregore is strengthened by time and experience, and the will and intention of good men. The strength of the egregore is patent in the effect the ritual has on the candidate, and effect that cannot be accounted for simply in the execution of the ritual itself.

---

[7] *Spiritual Influences and Egregores* by René Guénon, in *Initiation and Spiritual Realization,* cit. p119

We have all experienced the thrill, the exhilaration of the initiation, and the emotional high that carries us for days afterward as the flame is kindled in our breast. This is the spirit the egregore connects us with that fills us and carries us. It is this spirit that breathes in us, inspires us with brotherly love, relief, truth and charity.

The spirit is from the divine. The egregore is the psychic link between the mortal to the spirit. The mason is inspired by the breath of the spirit.

And thus: Freemasonry.

THE CHAIN OF UNION

By: Giovanni Lombardo

There are more things in heaven and earth, Horatio than are dreamt of in your philosophy.
(Shakespeare, Hamlet, I, V. 166-7)

Freemasonry is a "Peculiar Morality, veiled in allusion and illustrated by symbols." Of course, there are many types of symbols, there are visual symbols, pictures, oral symbols, which primarily make up speech, and demonstrated or enacted symbols. The Chain of Union is an "enacted" symbol, that is, a rite by gesture.

Generally, it is formed at closing a lodge, and usually only in the first-degree. Some do it immediately before the closing, others after, and some as a part of the ritual of initiation where is it done in an evocative manner: Immediately after closing the works, the novice is placed "between the pillars" where he is able to see the formation of the chain. After it is formed, by order of the master, the circle is opened towards the West so the candidate, crossing the threshold, is welcomed into and becomes an integral part of it. The chain is closed, locked "with force and vigour", having assimilated the new ring in an almost organic way.

The Chain of Union is ancient, going back to the *Compagnonnage* — the 12th century French stonemason corporation — where it is known as "alliance's chain." Francisco Ariza thinks this ritual acted as support for a sacred invocation, it being a collective practice of "enchantment". Enchantment is a sacred invocation, and is just a mean to activate a memory of what is already inside the agent, awakening his inner faculties.[1]

---

[1] *El símbolo y el rito masónico de la cadena de unión*, in *Symbolos* n. 3, 1992, pp. 14-5

To this end Bro. René Guénon wrote:

"By the comparison they allow, these considerations will make it easier to understand what we will now say about 'incantation'. It is essential to note that what we designate with this name has absolutely nothing to do with the magical practices to which the name is sometimes given; besides, we have already said enough about magic so that no confusion should be possible and no further comment necessary.

In contrast to prayer, the incantation we spoke of is not a petition and does not even presuppose the existence of anything outward, which every petition necessarily supposes, because outwardness cannot be understood except in relation to the individual, which is here precisely surpassed. It is an aspiration of the being toward the Universal in order to obtain what we might call in somewhat 'theological' language a spiritual grace, that is, essentially an inward illumination that can naturally be more or less complete according to the case.

Here the action of the spiritual influence must be seen in its pure state, if one can speak thus; instead of seeking to make it descend, as in prayer, the being tends on the contrary to rise toward it. The incantation thus defined as an entirely inward operation in principle can nonetheless in many cases expressed and 'supported' outwardly by words or gestures that constitute initiatic rites, such as the *mantra* in the Hindu tradition or the *dhikr* in the Islamic tradition, which must be thought of as a producing rhythmic vibrations that reverberate throughout a more or less extensive domain in the indefinite series of the states of the being.

Whether the result obtained be more or less complete, the final goal is always the realization in oneself of 'Universal Man' by the perfect communication of all these states in proper and harmonious hierarchy and in an integral expansion, both in 'amplitude' and 'exaltation', that is, both as to the horizontal expansion of the modalities of each state and the vertical superposition of the different states, according to the geometrical figuration that we have explained in detail elsewhere."[2]

* * *

Let us now examine the shape of the chain. The Brethren remove their gloves and gather themselves, forming a circular frame around to the Tracing Board or altar in lodges where the altar is in the center of the lodge. Each Brother crosses his right arm on the left so to form a symbolic cross of Saint Andrew, joining hands to those of his neighbour from both sides, so that one's right-hand grips one another's left: the former 'covers' and the latter 'supports'. In the Far-East tradition the right side matches to the yang, or the masculine element, it being 'the way of Heaven', while the left one is that of yin, feminine, representing the Earth: 'Heaven covers and Earth holds'. For some reading this, a recollection of the due guard of the first degree will also illustrate the concept.

Man has to interpret the terms as complementary, rather than opposite, bearing in mind that "in all manifested things [other than Heaven and Earth] there is no yang without yin and no yin without yang, for everything by nature partakes simultaneously of both Heaven and Earth".[3] This is the duality of man and masonry.

The Master Mason, perfectly balanced, is always 'in the middle', mediator between the two elements, and thus becomes the third leg of the triad, that which joins the duad

---

[2] René Guénon, *Perspectives on Initiation*, Sophia Perennis, Gent, NY, chap. XXIV, pp. 163-164
[3] René Guénon, *The Great Triad*, Quinta Essentia, Cambridge, 1991 p. 31

into a triad and thus becomes the monad. I am reminded of the Masonic formula, according to which the initiate must know how 'to discern the light in the darkness (the yang in the yin) and the darkness in the light (the yin in the yang)'.

As the brothers' hands are joined to form the circle, each Brother unites his own heels so to form a square and opens the points, in order to let them contact the ones of his neighbours. The chin is on to the chest, the eyes closed and everybody concentrates on "the Worshipful Master's intent", even if it remains undisclosed. The Brethren are silent and meditative. After some time the Worshipful Master shakes his arms three times and so do all the Brethren and thereafter let hands loose and "break" the Chain. If the works are still to be finished, the Brethren return to their places.

* * *

The Chain of Union is a continuous physical symbol and as such, it reminds us of the sign of the Pythagoreans, which had to be traced in a continuous way. From that man can deduce that the Chain testifies in a tangible way to the invisible tie that joins all the members of a lodge, and truly, in a more general way, to all Freemasons withersoever dispersed.

The reference to the Universal within the chain is clear if we imagine it as being seen from above. Its shape is roughly a circle, the centre of which is shown clearly. Therefore, if on the one hand the circle represents the temporal and the dynamic expression of the initiatic chain — the world of the Manifestation — while on the other hand the point recalls the permanent origin, or the Immutable Being.

Last, but not the least, we must examine another aspect of the Chain, which refers itself to the interaction between the 'thick' and the 'subtle'. From physics we know that each geometric solid figure causes waves which vary according to the form of the figure. These waves are known as form-waves, or shape-waves, which can be measured according to their vibratory frequency.

Egyptians knew of this phenomenon, and in fact used it to protect the Kings' chambers by emitting waves which are vibrating in the electrical phase, harmful for living entities: man commonly speaks about the "curse of Tutankhamen". To the contrary, churches and pyramids emit waves, which vibrate in the magnetic phase, so they are favourable for men. In ancient times, Freemasons were aware of this peculiarity and therefore they protected their constructions through the cornerstone, which has a trapezoidal shape.

There is no 'magick' in this, no witchcraft, just an acknowledgement of physical facts. The interpretation of their effect is subject to discussion, to be sure. However, there is nothing in Masonic ritual of which we should be ashamed. Initiates reject the artificial distinction between physics and metaphysics; they are aware that "rites and symbols are fundamentally only two aspects of a single reality, which is, after all, none other than the 'correspondence' that binds everything together through all the degrees of existence in such a way our human state can enter into communication with or at least dimly perceive, the higher states of being."[4]

Let's turn back to the Chain. The Worshipful Master, as the focus and exciter, by initiating the chain starts the energy, which passes to his neighbour and so on around the chain. The energy so amassed and strengthened comes back to the Worshipful Master and therefore launched to the 'astral', from which it turns back on earth, like a rocket on the target, to carry out the "intent" which was mentally expressed by the Worshipful Master at the beginning of the ceremony. Thus the ceremony projects the will of the Brethren.

---

[4] René Guénon, *Rite and Symbol*, in *Perspectives on Initiation*, chap. XVI, p. 114

THE MASONIC DRESS

By: Giovanni Lombardo

The Masonic dress of Brothers in lodge essentially consists of the plain white lambskin apron, and white gloves. Both of these items have ritual and symbolic significance to a Mason. In addition, officers wear collars with declare their station. From these collars depend what we refer to as Jewels; the Square of the Master, the Level of the Senior Warden, the Plumb of the Junior Warden, the Crossed Quills of the Secretary, the Crossed Keys of the Treasurer, the Harp of the Organist, the Square and Compass surrounding the shining sun of the Senior Deacon, the square and compass surrounding the Crescent Mood of the Junior Deacon, the Cornucopia of the Stewards and the Sword of the Tyler.

Each of these jewels has ritual and symbolic significance of their own, in addition to declaring which officer is which. And on one brother, the master of the lodge, is the hat, usually a top hat, though in some jurisdictions it can be a cowboy hat, a beret, or a hat chosen by the master. Of course, in some jurisdictions, the master does not wear a hat at all.

We are taught in ritual that in ancient times, stonecutters wore a lambskin apron, longer than the ones in use today. These aprons were strong enough to protect the wearer from splinters, scrapes and keep their clothing from being soiled while working in stone. This danger no longer exists as we are speculative, not operative masons, so the apron today is symbolic. It represents the purity of conduct so essentially necessary to gain admission into the great lodge above. As with everything in Masonry, the apron also has a deeper and more esoteric meaning.

The apron is most often made of lambskin (or a reasonable facsimile) though there are also aprons available in many lodges that are cloth or even silk. Many believe that the lambskin apron should still bear the wool, this being an animal fibre, in an esoteric sense, it can then act as insulator.

The apron's shape is that of a square, with a triangular flap on it. The square symbolizes the matter while the triangle, the vertex of which is up, reminds us of the alchemic symbol of fire, thus symbolizing the zeal that pushes Freemasons toward heaven, the siege of the Supreme Being.

The apron also represents a Broached Thurnel, when the flap is turned up. This is particularly symbolic of several things in most United States Rituals. The Broached Thurnel is a symbol that has been dropped from the ritual, while it is retained in the way an Entered Apprentice is taught to wear his apron.

The apron covers the genitalia's region, thus isolating it from the rest of the body. In order to work properly to the glory of the Grand Architect, as we are taught, all Freemasons must learn to subdue his passions within proper bounds.

Entered Apprentices wear their apron keeping the flap up: this further precaution is to protect the epigastrium, the part of human body which is immediately over the stomach. This is where the *manipura chakra* is located. The passions' *chakra* corresponds to the solar plexus. The Entered Apprentice's job is to learn to subdue his passions, for like the youth the degree symbolizes, the Entered Apprentice is considered unable to control incoming energies satisfactorily. Therefore, it is expedient that they protect themselves and the brethren adequately.

We have already noticed that the apron of the Entered Apprentice recalls the Broached Thurnel. This is a symbol which pertains to masters: the matter – the square – is turned into the spiritual: the triangle. The entered apprentice wears the apron with the top turned up to act as a 'reminder', showing to him the task which he must carry out. Conversely, Fellow Crafts and Master Masons keep the flap down: this means that the mental and the spiritual, respectively, closely interact with matter, as it happens in the symbolism of David's star.

White gloves are the other item of the Masonic dress. In Italy, it is compulsory to wear them in each lodge's meeting, as long as the meeting lasts. The only exception is when the Brethren form the union's chain at the close of lodge. In that case, hands must be bare so that the subtle energies of the Brethren can circulate more easily.

Gloves are symbol of purity: being hands symbol of human actions. Wearing the gloves reminds us of that purity and innocence with which we must work, performing only pure acts. Gloves, however, are also a tool: in the Temple everything is sacred, so nothing can be touched, but by pure hands.

It is worth noting that in old catholic liturgy, only popes and bishops could wear white gloves, thus evoking the hands of Jacob, that were covered with "the skins of the kids of the goats".[1] We know that the name "Jacob" means "the substitute", hence the idea of regeneration, of a new man that takes the place of the old one, like light which drives darkness away.

According the ritual of Grande Oriente d'Italia, the Entered Apprentice receives two pairs of gloves: one for himself and the other one for his "perfect lunar polarity". He should give that other pair to the woman in whom he bears the utmost esteem. It is difficult to determine when this practice started, though there is a small hint in Pérau in 1742, though it is thought this use is far older.[2] Masonic history informs us that Bro. Goethe gifted his second pair of gloves to Mrs. Von Stein, remarking that "even if the gift was seemingly poor, nonetheless it had a particular feature, that is, it can be given by a Freemason "only once in his life".

---

[1] Genesis: 27,16
[2] Gabriel Louis Pérau, *L'ordre des Francs-Maçons trahi et les secret des Mopses révelé,* 1742, quoted by Irène Manguy, *La Symbolique maçonnique du troisième millénaire,* Paris 2001. Italian translation 2004, p. 100, footnote 11.

Master Masons should cover their head when they work in the third degree. The reason of this use lies in the esoteric feature of hair. Henry Allaix wrote that hair works like a receiving set, while beard and moustache are thought to emit energy.[3] In ancient times, Christian monks received a tonsure, which removed the hair on their heads, but they did not shave. So the master covers his head thus showing he refuses any external influences...

Other interpretations are however possible. From the ritual we are learned that the Lodge begins to work when it  is properly tiled. On the other side, every human body is the "temple of the Holy Ghost"[4], so the Master Mason who covers his head actually tiles his own temple. Still today, in their temples where they are appearing before G-D, observant Jews wear the *kippah*, and in Italy many Master Masons do the same.

Last, but not the least, few words about the tunic. (fig. 1) In Italy, during the two world wars, Freemasons wore it. The tunic is black, and its colour reminds us of the importance of the hermetic work's phase which is called *Crow's head*, or *nigredo*.[5] There is a deep esoteric meaning in wearing the tunic, for it teaches the brethren to give up vanity and any outer difference. In wearing the tunic, they are really meeting on the level.

As is taught in the first degree, when the candidate is neither naked nor clad, it is not the outer qualifications that make a man a mason, but the inner. The tunic makes all equal. The tunic also resembles the symbol of death, the grim reaper. In this sense, the tunic represents to the candidate the death of profanity, the rebirth into the new light.

---

[3] *Introduction à l'étude de la Magie*, 1936
[4] I Corinthians, 6: 19
[5] See *The Chamber of Reflection*

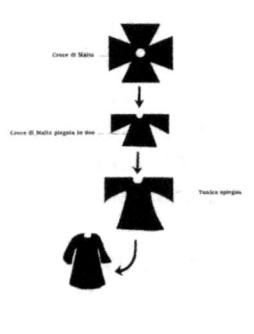

The candidate is visually reminded of the death of the old, and thereby the rebirth, into the new.

Today, the tunic is worn by the Marshall when he escorts the Candidate into the Temple for the ceremony of initiation. The tunic's shape stems from the cross of Malta, being a folded cross. (fig. 2)

We know that the cross can be inscribed in the square, symbol of matter, but also in the circle, symbol of spirit, thus alluding to the transformation which is gained by the initiate who has purified his heart and his mind and is therefore worthy to "ascend into the hill of Lord".[6]

---

[6] Psalm XXIV

www.ingramcontent.com/pod-product-compliance
Lightning Source LLC
Chambersburg PA
CBHW070456100426
42743CB00010B/1650